DINOSAURS

DINOSAURS
An Illustrated History
by Edwin H. Colbert

A Dembner Book

Hammond Incorporated

MAPLEWOOD, NEW JERSEY

A Dembner Book
Produced by Red Dembner Enterprises Corp.,
1841 Broadway, New York, N.Y. 10023
Editor: S. Arthur Dembner
Executive Editor: Anna Dembner
Art Director: Hermann Strohbach

Printed in the United States of America.

Library of Congress Cataloging in Publication Data

Colbert, Edwin Harris, 1905–
    Dinosaurs, an illustrated history.

    "A Dembner book."
    Bibliography: p.
    Includes index.
    1. Dinosaurs.   I. Title.
QE862.D5C673   1983   567.9′1   82-23273
ISBN 0-8437-3332-2
ISBN 0-8437-1075-6 (classics)

CONTENTS

Acknowledgments

The writing of a book such as this represents much more than the single effort of the author. Above all, a book of this nature owes its being primarily to the labors of many dedicated workers throughout the world and throughout the years. During the past century and a half men and women have been searching for, digging up, and studying the fossils of dinosaurs in lands far and wide, to accumulate and interpret bones now turned to stone, footprints, petrified eggs, and other evidence that taken together have revealed the long history of the rulers of Mesozoic continents. The first and greatest debt is to these hunters and students of the dinosaurs.

More immediately the author is indebted to institutions and people that have contributed in a direct way to the composition of this book. First I take great pleasure in acknowledging my debt of gratitude to the American Museum of Natural History in New York, where I spent forty years of my scientific career, and where, among other things, I had the privilege of supervising the revisions and modernization of the two great dinosaur halls. It was indeed my good fortune to spend much time during those forty years in studying the fossil collections in the museum and thus learning something about vertebrate evolution.

Again, I would like to acknowledge my gratitude to the Museum of Northern Arizona in Flagstaff, where for the past fourteen years I have been able to continue my studies of fossil vertebrates.

Next I would like to express my appreciation to numerous friends and colleagues who have generously helped with advice, and with permission to use some of the fruits of their labors.

It affords me particular pride to thank two of my former students, Dr. John H. Ostrom of Yale University and Dr. Dale Russell of the National Museum of Canada, for their kindness in making available illustrations and other materials from their published works. In the same vein I wish to express my gratitude to Dr. Alan J. Charig of the British Museum (Natural History), Dr. James A. Jensen of Brigham Young University, Dr. Nicholas Hotton III of the Smithsonian Institution, Drs. A. W. Crompton and Farish A. Jenkins, Jr., of Harvard University, Dr. Donald Baird of Princeton University, Dr. William A. Clemens of the University of California in Berkeley, Dr. David Archibald of Yale University, Dr. Samuel P. Welles and Mr. Robert A. Long of the University of California in Berkeley, Dr. Zofia Kielan-Jaworowska of the Polish Academy of Science in Warsaw, and Dr. Anthony Thulborn of the University of Queensland, in Brisbane, Australia.

Special thanks are due to Miss Charlotte Holton of the American Museum of Natural History in New York for her helpful assistance in clarifying some difficult references. I wish particularly to thank my wife, Margaret Colbert, who made many illustrations specifically for this volume.

Finally I wish on behalf of my wife and myself to express our gratitude and deep appreciation for the invaluable assistance given to us by the editors, Mr. S. Arthur Dembner (who directed the project) and Mrs. Anna Dembner. They devoted innumerable long hours to the production of the book. If the reader finds the writing herein felicitous and accurate and the pages pleasing to the eye, it is in no small way owing to the experienced efforts of the Dembners.

Edwin H. Colbert
Flagstaff, Arizona
February 21, 1983

PREFACE

The dinosaurs, rulers of the continents for more that one hundred million years until their extinction some sixty-five million years ago, have been known to Man for little more than a century and a half. As we shall see, a dinosaur bone was described as long ago as 1677 (mistakenly identified as from an elephant, brought to Britain by the Romans), but it was not until 1842 that the word *Dinosauria* was invented by Sir Richard Owen, the famous English anatomist and paleontologist. Today dinosaurs are known and appreciated by people throughout the world, and the word *dinosaur* is firmly entrenched within scores of languages.

This worldwide interest in the dinosaurs is one result of excavations in the field and studies in the laboratory, vigorously prosecuted only since about the middle of the nineteenth century. Thus the dinosaurian branch of paleontology (paleontology being the comprehensive study of ancient life) is a comparatively young scientific discipline. It is much younger than biology as such, which was studied by the ancient Greeks; or of geology as

such, which in its more primitive aspects was practiced to a degree by the medieval miners of Europe; or even of paleontology as such, which was being established during the eighteenth century. It is not as young as genetics within the biological world, or as geophysics within the geological world. Nevertheless the study of dinosaurs is a fairly recent addition to the great body of human knowledge. For many people it is a very exciting study.

Within the past decade or so there has been an unprecedented surge of interest in dinosaurs, not only among the public but also within the scientific community. There are several reasons why this should be so. Part of the interest is owing to discoveries of hitherto unknown dinosaurs in many regions of the earth and their display in museums. Part of it is owing to an increased awareness among paleontologists, and among other scientists as well, of what can be learned from the study of dinosaurs.

For long years the dinosaurs were considered by numerous paleontologists as remarkable but not especially important extinct animals. Many of the dinosaurs were giants, it is true, and many of them show unusual features of structural anatomy. But, so it was reasoned, they were dead ends. They did not lead anywhere; they did not give rise to later animals that carried evolutionary lineages to the present day. (Perhaps some of them did; we shall look into that subsequently.) All in all they were frequently viewed as "gee-whiz" fossils—interesting and fun to look at, but none the less on a side line in the general scheme of things.

In contrast to this attitude much attention was given to the therapsids, the mammal-like reptiles that lived before the supremacy of the dinosaurs, and among which some were directly ancestral to the mammals. Much attention was given to the early mammals, descended from certain therapsids, and among which were to be found the roots of mammalian evolution, from which roots certain lineages lead to Man. Here, it seemed, were the fruitful paleontological fields to be tilled and cultivated.

Recently, however, many paleontologists and zoologists, not to mention geologists and practitioners within other scientific spheres, have come to see the dinosaurs as important extinct animals from which much is to be learned. These ancient reptiles are seen as viable animals—very much alive to a careful and discerning student. From the dinosaurs we are learning new lessons about the problems of structure in giants, about the possible physiology of such beasts, about their relationships to the world in which they lived, about their distributions and the bearing of such distributions on the past arrangements of the continents, about various aspects of evolution, and about that perennial question: why did they become extinct? Studies of these subjects and many more, initially highly technical, have frequently been presented in generally understood terms, creating an immense amount of public interest. An example is the furor over the question of "warm-blooded" dinosaurs.

A result of all this has been a recent plethora of books about dinosaurs—and here is one more. Perhaps there is room for all of these books, because each will present the subject in its own particular way. This present book is an attempt to portray the natural history of the dinosaurs: their beginnings, their evolutionary development, their role in the world they inhabited, and their demise. It is a very large subject and can only be outlined within the confines of a book such as this. It is to be hoped that the outline will be interesting and useful, and will help to introduce the reader to the world as it was long ago—a world very different from the one in which we live.

DINOSAURS

DISCOVERY AND STUDY

On a sunny spring morning in 1822 Mary Ann Mantell was strolling along a country road near Lewes, a small city near the Channel Coast, south of London. Her husband, Dr. Gideon Algernon Mantell, a Lewes physician, was inside a nearby house attending one of his patients, and Mrs. Mantell, who had accompanied him on his morning call to enjoy the fresh air of the spring countryside, had alighted from their carriage in order to observe in an intimate way some of the wild flowers and grasses, newly sprung from the awakening earth. As she walked down the road she saw a pile of rocks that had been dumped near the road's edge, to be used for repairing the roadway. And enclosed within some of the rocks she saw some objects shining in the morning sunlight, which on closer examination seemed to be large, fossilized teeth. All unwit-

The restoration of *Iguanodon* done by Waterhouse Hawkins under the supervision of Richard Owen, as it appears today in Sydenham, London.

11

tingly Mary Ann Mantell had become one of the first persons to discover a dinosaur.

Gideon Mantell (1790–1852) was something more than the average medical practitioner; he was intensely interested in the fossils that were being found in the ancient Cretaceous* sediments of the South Downs of England. Indeed, Mantell was just completing a book entitled *The Fossils of the South Downs, or Illustrations of the Geology of Sussex*, illustrated by his wife.

Mary Ann knew that Gideon would be interested in these strange, new fossils, the likes of which she had never seen, so when he emerged from the house of his ailing patient she showed him the fossils that she had found, and he immediately became very excited. He realized that these were the teeth of some hitherto unknown plant-eating ani-

---

*As shown on the geologic time chart (page 56) the dinosaurs lived during the Mesozoic Era of earth history. This span of geologic time is divided into three periods, of which the Triassic Period is the oldest, the Jurassic Period of intermediate age, and the Cretaceous Period the youngest. The beginning of the Triassic Period is dated at about two hundred thirty million years ago, the end of the Cretaceous Period at about sixty-five million years ago. The dinosaurs appeared during late Triassic time, perhaps two hundred million years ago, and continued to the end of the Cretaceous Period.

mal, but what kind of an animal it might have been was a mystery. Nevertheless he included some pictures of the teeth, drawn at the last minute by Mary Ann, in his forthcoming book, which was published in May, 1822.

Mantell soon located the quarry from which the rocks containing the teeth had been excavated; it was near Cuckfield, in the Tilgate Forest, about a dozen miles to the northwest of Lewes. There he found more teeth, as well as some scattered skeletal remains. Then began a protracted bit of early paleontological detective work in an effort to identify the animal represented by the teeth and bones. The fossils were submitted to Baron Georges Cuvier in Paris, the preeminent paleontologist and comparative anatomist of his day, who first identified one of the teeth as belonging to a fossil rhinoceros, and subsequently identified some of the other remains as of an ancient hippopotamus. These early gropings into an unknown ancient world were described by Mantell in the following words:

Soon after my first discovery of bones of colossal reptiles in the strata of Tilgate Forest, some teeth of a very remarkable character particularly excited my curiosity, for they were wholly unlike any that had previously come under my observation; even the quarrymen

Left: Gideon Algernon Mantell, the English physician who described *Iguanodon*. This picture is from his later years, when he was completely devoted to the study of fossils—especially dinosaurs.

Right: Mary Ann Mantell, who found the teeth of *Iguanodon* in 1822.

English gentlemen in top hats, and their assistants in less formal dress, collecting fossils early in the nineteenth century.

Baron Georges Cuvier, the French anatomist and pale-ontologist whose advice concerning the fossil remains of *Iguanodon* was sought by Gideon Mantell.

accustomed to collect the remains of fishes, shells, and other objects embedded in the rocks, had not observed fossils of this kind; and until shown some specimens which I had extracted from a block of stone, were not aware of the presence of such teeth in the stone they were constantly breaking up for the roads.

The first specimen that arrested my attention was a large tooth, which from the worn, smooth and oblique surface of the crown, evidently belonged to an herbivorous animal; and so entirely resembled in form the corresponding part of an incisor of a large pachyderm ground down by use, that I was much embarrassed to account for its presence in such ancient strata; in which, according to all geological experience, no fossil remains of mammalia would ever be discovered; and as no known existing reptiles are capable of masticating their food, I could not venture to assign the tooth in question to a saurian.

As my friend Mr. (now Sir Charles) Lyell was about to visit Paris, I availed myself of the opportunity of submitting it to the examination of Baron Cuvier, with whom I had the high privilege of corresponding; and, to my astonishment, learned from my friend that M. Cuvier, without hesitation, pronounced it to be an upper incisor of a rhinoceros.

I had previously taken this tooth, and some other specimens, to a meeting of the Geological Society in London, and shown them to Dr. Buckland, Mr. Conybeare, Mr. Clift, and other eminent men who were present, but without any satisfactory result: in fact I was discouraged by the remark that the teeth were of no particular interest, as there could be little doubt they belonged either to some large fish allied to the *Anarhicas lupus*, or wolf-fish, the crowns of whose incisors are of a prismatic form, or were mammalian teeth obtained from a diluvial deposit. Dr. Wollaston alone supported my opinion that I had discovered the teeth of an unknown herbivorous reptile, and encouraged me to continue my researches.

And as if to add to the difficulty of solving the enigma, some metacarpal bones which I soon discovered in the same quarry, and forwarded to Paris, were declared to belong to a species of hippopotamus. Subsequently a dermal horn or tubercle from the same stratum was declared by competent authorities to be the lesser horn of a rhinoceros; and Dr. Buckland, with the generous kindness which marked his character, wrote to guard me against venturing to publish that these teeth, bones and horn, were found in the 'Iron-sand formation', with which the Tilgate beds were then classed, as there could be no doubt they belonged to the superficial diluvium: and as the upper beds of the conglomerate in which these first specimens were found was only covered by loam and vegetable earth, there was no clear stratigraphical evidence to support a contrary opinion. (Mantell, quoted in Sidney Spokes, *Gideon Algernon Mantell: Surgeon and Geologist* [London: J. Bale, Sons, and Danielson, 1927], pages 20–21.)

Mantell was not satisfied. So he took his specimens to London, where he wished to compare them with teeth and bones in the Hunterian Museum of the Royal College of Surgeons, which housed an extensive collection of all kinds of animals large and small, fossil and recent. For hours he searched through seemingly innumerable drawers containing teeth and bones, and had almost reached a point of despair in his attempt to find anything that resembled his fossils. It so happened, however, that a young man named Samuel Stutchbury was also studying at the Hunterian Museum on that particu-

lar day. Mantell showed him the fossils, and Stutchbury immediately saw a resemblance between the fossil teeth and those of a Central American iguana lizard, which he was studying. When Stutchbury showed some iguana teeth to Mantell, the physician-paleontologist, too, recognized a similarity between the ancient fossil and the modern lizard. (How often are discoveries in science determined by chance events—in this case an unexpected meeting with a stranger.)

Consequently Mantell described his fossils—he now was certain that they represented an extinct reptile—and his paper was published in the Philosophical Transactions of the Royal Society of London for 1825. He named the fossil *Iguanodon* (*iguana* plus *odon*, meaning tooth; therefore "iguana-tooth"). Thus a dinosaur, still not recognized as a dinosaur for the idea of dinosaurs had not as yet been born, came into the consciousness of mankind.

Dr. Buckland, mentioned by Mantell in his account quoted above of the discovery of *Iguanodon* and the first attempts to establish its relationships, was William Buckland (born in 1784), first professor of geology at Oxford University, and dean of Christ Church. He was one of those eccentric characters that graced the English scene during the nineteenth century, a man of learning and a divine who delighted in unexpected and sometimes astonishing quips and actions. For example, a bear named Tiglath Pilaser, a pet of Buckland's son, Frank, was for some time a resident at Christ Church, where on festive occasions he was dressed in a cap and gown,

in which costume he attended garden parties and other academic celebrations.

At about the time that Mantell was preoccupied with his fossils, Buckland became interested in a large fossil jaw containing sharp, blade-like teeth, and in other bones as well. The fossils had been found in Jurassic sediments at Stonesfield in Oxfordshire, evidently during the early years of the nineteenth century, for Cuvier had seen the jaw when he visited Oxford in 1818. No description of the materials had been published; but after having seen the fossils Mantell had found, Cuvier urged Buckland to describe the fossils at Oxford. Buckland did so in 1824, naming the animal *Megalosaurus* ("giant lizard").

Buckland was not, however, the originator of the name *Megalosaurus*. In 1822, the year in which Mary Ann and Gideon Mantell became involved with *Iguanodon*, the English physician and geologist James Parkinson (his name is memorialized by Parkinson's disease, which he identified) published a small book with a long title: *Outlines of Oryctology, An Introduction to the Study of Fossil Organic Remains especially of those found in the British Strata*, and in this book he made some mention of a fossil that he designated *Megalosaurus*. According to Parkinson: "It is found in the calcareous slate of Stonefield . . . Drawings have been made of the most essential parts of the animal, now in the Museum in Oxford; and it is hoped that a description may be shortly given to the public. The animal must in some instances, have attained a length of forty feet, and stood eight feet high." (Parkinson, quoted in

16

Sir Richard Owen as a young man. The foremost English anatomist of his day, first "superintendent" of the British Museum (Natural History) and an early authority on the dinosaurs. He invented the word *Dinosauria*.

W. E. Swinton, *The Dinosaurs* [New York: John Wiley and Sons, 1970], page 31.)

Parkinson's wish was soon fulfilled by Buckland's description. It seems probable, however, that the remains of dinosaurs had been seen long before the discoveries of *Iguanodon* and *Megalosaurus*, and it is not unlikely that ancient and medieval tales of giants may have been based in part upon the bones of dinosaurs, exposed by the erosion of rocks. One definite observation of a probable dinosaur bone goes back to seventeenth-century England, where the Reverend Robert Plot of Oxford described and figured a gigantic leg bone in 1677, which he thought "must have belonged to some greater *animal* than either an *Ox* or *Horse;* it must have been the *Bone* of some *Elephant*, brought hither during the Government of the *Romans* in *Britain*." (Swinton, page 26.)

Almost a century later Joshua Platt, also of Oxford, found three large fossil vertebrae and a leg bone, which latter specimen he described and illustrated. The brief description and figure were published in 1758, in the Philosophical Transactions of the Royal Society of London, at the behest of Mr. Peter Collinson, a fellow of the society. At the time it was commonly thought that the leg bone was from a victim of Noah's flood, but Platt concluded that perhaps it was a hippopotamus or rhinoceros bone.

It may be said that the bones described by Plot and by Platt were, as distinguished from other dinosaur bones found during early times, truly *discovered* in a scientific sense, because scientific discovery involves making something known through publication. "It has been well said that the date of a discovery is the date of its publication." (Leslie Alcock, *Arthur's Britain*, [Harmondsworth, Middlesex: Penguin Books, 1980], page 153.)

Advancing forward in time, a third specimen, *Hylaeosaurus*, was described by Mantell in 1832, to be added to *Iguanodon* and *Megalosaurus*. These described fossils, however, technically were not dinosaurs, because the concept of dinosaurs had not as yet been born. Rather they were extinct reptiles of large size.

It remained for another Englishman, Richard Owen (1804–1892), to bring the dinosaurs into being. Owen (subsequently Sir Richard), a personal friend of Queen Victoria and a sometime tutor of her numerous children, the leading comparative anatomist of England and a worthy successor to Cuvier, Hunterian professor at the Royal College of

Surgeons and conservator of the museum, eventually founder and first superintendent (as the title was then) of the British Museum (Natural History), had ample opportunities to become intimately acquainted with animals of all kinds, fossil and recent. As a result of his studies he realized that the large reptilian bones that had been unearthed in southern England were not to be equated with any modern reptiles. Consequently, in 1841, at the meetings of the British Association for the Advancement of Science, in Plymouth, he suggested that these fossils represent a separate group of reptiles, now extinct. His proposal was published in the *Proceedings* of the association, in 1842, page 103.

The combination of such characters, some, as the sacral bones, altogether peculiar among Reptiles, others borrowed, as it were, from groups now distinct from each other, and all manifested by creatures far surpassing in size the largest of existing reptiles, will, it is presumed, be deemed sufficient ground for establishing a distinct tribe or suborder of Saurian Reptiles, for which I would propose the name of *Dinosauria*.

(As we shall see, Owen's original definition was

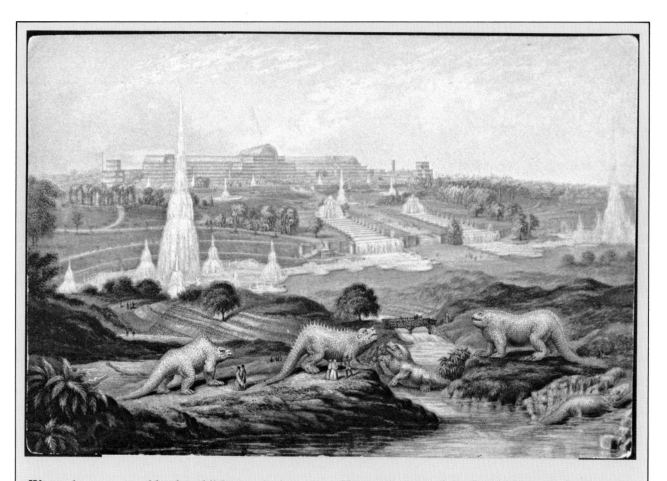

We see here a rare old colored lithograph showing the grounds of the Crystal Palace at Sydenham, in southeast London. In the background is the palace; in the foreground are some of the life-size restorations, made by Waterhouse Hawkins under the direction of Richard Owen, being examined by some Victorian ladies and gentlemen.

Here are some of the first visions of dinosaurs as they were thought to have appeared, *Megalosaurus* being the pair at the left, *Iguanodon,* the pair below and to the right of the near-distant bridge. Crystal Palace subsequently was destroyed by fire, but the models remain and are maintained, for the delectation of modern visitors.

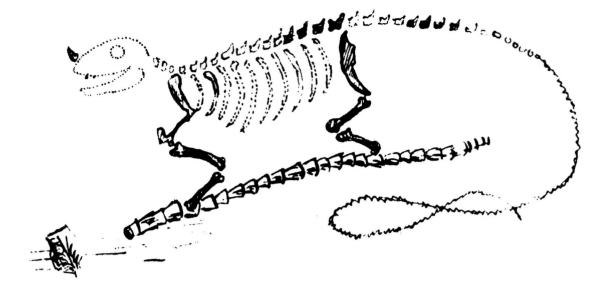

subsequently modified to some extent; not all dinosaurs are gigantic or even large, and they are not contained within a single group, but rather belong to two distinct orders of reptiles.)

So a new word came into the English language, and indeed into any number of languages throughout the world. It is of course the word *dinosaur* (from the Greek *deinos*, terrible, and *sauros*, lizard). What was an obscure scientific term, applied to a few incomplete fossils in 1842, has within the span of a century and a half become a well-recognized vernacular word, widely used by people around the world.

In the realm of discovery it always helps to know what one is looking for. Richard Owen brought dinosaurs into being in 1842, and once it was realized that there were dinosaurs in the earth the discoveries of these ancient reptiles began to increase in a dramatic fashion as the years went by. Furthermore there were discoveries in regions other than southern England, indeed to such an extent that within three or four decades after Owen's definition of the Dinosauria, the center for dinosaurian discoveries and research had shifted from Europe to North America. But before embarking on this phase of our story, let us take a last look at Richard Owen and the dinosaurs.

This brings in the famous Crystal Palace of London and a gentleman named Waterhouse Hawkins. In 1851 the Crystal Palace had been erected in Hyde Park—politically and sociologically the first great world fair, and architecturally the first great modular structure, built of iron and glass. In 1854 the Crystal Palace was dismantled and moved to Sydenham, a spacious setting then on the outskirts of the great city. Here it was planned to construct life-size restorations of various extinct animals, to be placed in natural settings on the Sydenham grounds, the work to be accomplished by Mr. Hawkins under Owen's expert supervision. The project was pursued with dedicated application by Owen and Hawkins, to such a degree that Owen, for his part, spent almost all of his time during 1854 on this task. The models were constructed by Hawkins out of concrete and tile, which made them impervious to the damp climate of England, and were painted in colors assumed to be those of the living animals. For the Victorian visitors to Sydenham these evocations of life long since extinct were indeed impressive, and they still are. For although the Crystal Palace is now gone (it was destroyed by fire a half-century ago) the Waterhouse Hawkins creations remain for the enjoyment of modern sightseers.

Among the extinct animals at Sydenham are Gideon Mantell's *Iguanodon* and *Hylaeosaurus*, both reconstructed on the rather scanty evidence that existed in 1854. Owen supposed that *Iguanodon* was a bulky, quadrupedal reptile with a horn on its nose, and that is what can be seen today at Sydenham. With the discovery of complete skeletons of this dinosaur in Belgium in 1878 it became apparent that *Iguanodon* was a rather upright bipedal dinosaur, while the supposed nasal horn turned out to be a large spike on the first digit, or thumb, of this interesting reptile.

There is a postscript to the story of Waterhouse Hawkins and his restorations of extinct animals. In 1868 Hawkins, who was then in the United States, was invited to make a series of restorations, similar to those at Sydenham, to be displayed in the newly created Central Park of New York. Hawkins was delighted, and work commenced. The Central Park Commission had made elaborate plans for a

Mantell's first crude reconstruction of *Iguanodon*, which he then envisioned as a sort of gigantic lizard. He placed the spike borne by the thumb on the nose, a misconception that was to prevail until the discovery of complete skeletons in Belgium, in 1878.

The "Paleozoic Museum" was to have been an iron and glass structure, modeled somewhat in the style of the Crystal Palace, but of course on a much smaller scale, and was to have been located in Central Park, New York, near Eighth Avenue and opposite Sixty-third Street. It was never built but elaborate plans were made, and Waterhouse Hawkins with the aid of assistants labored hard on the models that were to be displayed inside. In this hopeful projection of the planned exhibit we see on the left the Cretaceous dinosaur *Hadrosaurus* standing high on its hind limbs, propped up by a strong tail, and being attacked by a carnivorous dinosaur. Another hadrosaur reclines peacefully in the foreground, eyeing a plesiosaur that seems to have come up on a beach. In the rear are two other dinosaurian carnivores contending for possession of their prey. The scale of these dinosaurs as compared with the Victorian New Yorkers shows that the extinct reptiles were restored to more than ample dimension.

To the right are some extinct mammals: ground sloths, a mastodon, and two armadillo-like glyptodonts—all animals that lived many millions of years after the dinosaurs had become extinct.

One wonders what the eventual fate of the Paleozoic Museum might have been, had it been built.

Joseph Leidy, the Philadelphia anatomist and paleontologist, with a leg bone of *Hadrosaurus* discovered at Haddonfield, New Jersey.

gave to them the name of *Hadrosaurus foulkii*. *Hadrosaurus*, one of the duck-billed dinosaurs, and the first dinosaur to be described from a reasonably complete skeleton, is related in a general way to *Iguanodon*. Leidy, having much of the skeleton before him, was able to interpret his dinosaur much more accurately than had been possible for Owen working with the fragments of *Iguanodon:*

The great disproportion of size between the fore and back parts of the skeleton of *Hadrosaurus*, leads me to suspect that this great extinct herbivorous lizard may have been in the habit of browsing, sustaining itself, kangaroo-like, in an erect position on its back extremities and tail. (Joseph Leidy, *Proceedings of the Academy of Natural Sciences* [Philadelphia, 1858], volume 10, page 217.)

And so, in the middle decade of the nineteenth century, two related dinosaurs came to life on the two sides of the Atlantic Ocean.

It is perhaps ironic that indications of dinosaurs in North America had been seen, collected, and studied many years before Leidy described *Hadrosaurus*, without those involved realizing that they were looking at the evidence of dinosaurs. These were Triassic dinosaur footprints, found in the Connecticut Valley.

Such footprints had been noted at least as early as 1804, at which time they were regarded as tracks made by large birds. Indeed, they were often referred to as the tracks of "Noah's ravens." In 1835 Edward Hitchcock, president of Amherst College, became interested in these tracks, which are abundantly preserved in the Triassic sandstones and shales up and down the Connecticut Valley, and so very much involved did he become with the footprints that he spent much of his time and energy, between 1835 and his death in 1864, in collecting, studying, and describing the fossils. As a result of his efforts there appeared in 1858 a large and handsome volume entitled *Ichnology of New England*, published by the state of Massachusetts. Subsequently, there appeared a supplementary volume, published the year after his death, with a preface addressed to Governor John A. Andrew of Massachusetts.

To the day of his death Hitchcock thought he was looking at the footprints of large birds, and that was how he descirbed them. Only later was it realized that these were dinosaur tracks; the first birds did not arise until millions of years after the end of Triassic time.

Perhaps the work of Hitchcock represents the first research on dinosaurs in North America, but it

The "Moody Foot Mark Quarry, South Hadley," Massachusetts. This illustration is taken from Edward Hitchcock's ambitious monograph *Ichnology of New England,* and shows footprints of Upper Triassic dinosaurs.

A view of fossil collecting in the badlands when western North America was "wild and woolly." The Yale expedition of 1873, led by Othniel Charles Marsh, a pioneer of paleontology in North America and the first director of the Yale Peabody Museum. Marsh is the second (upper) figure from the left.

Othniel Charles Marsh, first director of the Yale Peabody Museum, pioneer student of the dinosaurs, whose collections in the field and studies in the laboratory opened a vast new world to scientists and public in many lands.

Edward Drinker Cope of Philadelphia, anatomist, ichthyologist, herpetologist, and paleontologist, an erratic genius who collected and studied many dinosaurs from North America.

was in a way unknowing research. The fact remains that Leidy was the first to describe a dinosaur on this continent, knowing it to be a dinosaur.

The three pioneer vertebrate paleontologists in North America were Joseph Leidy, whom we have met, and Edward Drinker Cope (1840–1897) and Othniel Charles Marsh (1831–1899), with whom we will now become acquainted. Cope was a very well-to-do, if not a wealthy Philadelphian, the son of a Quaker shipowner who was much interested in philanthropic matters. Cope, whose mother died when he was a small boy, fortunately enjoyed the attentions of a sympathetic stepmother, so he grew up amidst a loving family in a spacious home. He showed a brilliant turn of mind at an early age. By the time he was six years old he was making drawings and writing some surprisingly knowledgeable notes about an ichthyosaur skeleton that he saw at the Philadelphia Academy of Natural Sciences, an institution with which he became associated in his later years. By the time he was in his teens he was carrying on truly professional studies of living and fossil reptiles. And by the time he was a mature man he was turning out scientific papers at a prodigious rate. He was a man of unexcelled brilliance who at the time of his death had published more than fourteen hundred scientific papers and monographs on fossil and recent vertebrates.

Marsh, who was born in Lockport, New York,

was the son of a not very successful farmer. Like Cope, he was motherless at an early age, but his boyhood was variously spent with family and relatives, so he lacked many of the advantages that were the privilege of Cope. Marsh, however, did have one asset—an exceedingly rich uncle. This uncle was George Peabody, the famous philanthropist, the man under whom J. P. Morgan was introduced to the world of finance. To make a long story short, Peabody supported Marsh as a student at Yale, where he became involved with fossils; subsequently Marsh persuaded his uncle to found and endow the Peabody Museum at that university, where Marsh spent all of his adult life.

Thus both Cope and Marsh were men of independent means; and as such they quickly became headstrong and demanding. As young men, just after the Civil War, they briefly were friends, but very soon they were implacable rivals engaged in a bitter feud. They were both involved in the scientific exploration of the Western Territories, where their respective field parties each year uncovered paleontological riches seemingly beyond the dreams of avarice. However Cope and Marsh were avaricious men—seeking not gold but fossils, for Cope's private collection and for Yale University. Soon all of the continent west of the Mississippi River was not big enough for the two of them. Each tried to beat the other with descriptions of new fos-

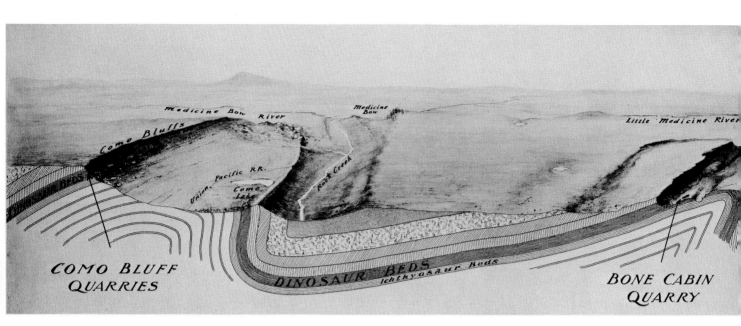

A section showing the folded strata at Como Bluff and Bone Cabin, Wyoming, where Yale University and the American Museum of Natural History made large collections of Upper Jurassic dinosaurs from the Morrison Formation.

sils. It even reached the point where Cope, for example, telegraphed descriptions of specimens to Philadelphia, for quick publication. It even reached the point where Marsh, for example, resorted to various subterfuges to prevent Cope from learning about his fossil localities. Even the men who worked for Cope and Marsh got dragged into the quarrel, whether they liked it or not.

The battle between Cope and Marsh reached such violent proportions that Leidy, a dignified and gentle person, abandoned his paleontological studies and turned to other things. He could not put up with the cross fire to which he was subjected.

Cope and Marsh collected and studied fossil vertebrates of many kinds, and high on their lists were the numerous dinosaurs that were being unearthed by their field parties. Their interests spanned all of the geological levels in which dinosaurs are found, but perhaps their most spectacular efforts were devoted to the excavation of the gigantic Upper Jurassic dinosaurs of the Morrison Formation—Cope principally at Canyon City, Colorado; Marsh at Como Bluff, Wyoming. (One of the men working for Marsh at Como Bluff was Arthur Lakes, an ex-En-

glishman, a graduate of Oxford, who made a series of primitive but charming watercolor sketches showing the work at that locality.)

Cope and his men had the temerity to visit the Como Bluff site in 1879, while Marsh's party was working there. There were some tense feelings between the rival parties, but Arthur Lakes discovered that Cope was perhaps not so bad as he had been depicted by Marsh. In his journal he had this to say:

The monstrum horrendum Cope has been and gone and I must say that what I saw of him I liked very much his manner is so affable and his conversation very agreeable. I only wish I could feel sure he had a sound reputation for honesty. (Lakes, quoted in John Ostrom and John S. McIntosh, *Marsh's Dinosaurs* [New Haven: Yale University Press, 1966], page 29.)

The Cope-Marsh feud was a disgraceful affair, yet since each man was trying to outdo his rival it did result in the discoveries of many paleontological treasures, including the skulls and skeletons of dinosaurs. These were described in numerous publications, Marsh with the aid of his assistants at

Mounting skeletons of *Iguanodon* from Bernissart, Belgium, in the medieval Chapel of St. George, Brussels. At that time the chapel was used as a laboratory by the Belgian Royal Museum.

A skeleton of *Iguanodon* from Bernissart, Belgium.

New Haven turning out massive monographs, some of which were unfinished at the time of his death. Cope, much more of a lone wolf than Marsh, published an incredible number of papers distinguished by trenchant insight. Today some of the dinosaurs that Marsh described are to be seen at the Peabody Museum of Yale University, while some of Cope's dinosaurs are on display at the American Museum of Natural History in New York, where the Cope collection is housed.

While Cope and Marsh were bringing to light the skeletons of various dinosaurs, long entombed in the Mesozoic sediments of the Rocky Mountain region, there was an accidental but very significant find of dinosaurs, deep within a coal mine in Belgium. The dinosaurs were *Iguanodon*, and they

were encountered in 1878 at a depth of 1,046 feet when some miners were developing a new gallery in an extensive mine near Bernissart. It was truly a fabulous concentration of *Iguanodon* skeletons, indeed so impressive that the director of the mine immediately informed the Belgian Royal Museum of Natural History, in Brussels, about the discovery. P. J. van Beneden, paleontologist at the museum, went to Bernissart to survey and evaluate what had been found. The result of his appraisal was to send M. De Pauw, director of the museum laboratory, to Bernissart, where he spent three long years at the mine, supervising the excavation of the dinosaur skeletons, which were subsequently studied and described by Louis Dollo, a scholar of prolific accomplishments. Having at hand more than thirty complete skeletons of varied sizes, Dollo was able to study *Iguanodon* in detail. He showed that this was a bipedal dinosaur, as years earlier Leidy had shown such to be the case for *Hadrosaurus*. As has been previously mentioned, it was revealed that the large spike that Owen had supposed to be a horn on the nose of *Iguanodon* was in fact a weapon carried on the thumb of this dinosaur. Today eleven mounted skeletons of *Iguanodon* from Bernissart may be seen at the museum in Brussels.

The initial work by Mantell, Buckland, and Owen, the excavation of the large concentration of *Iguanodon* skeletons in Belgium, and the unexcelled efforts of Cope and Marsh, resulting in the discovery of numerous varied dinosaurs throughout the western region of North America, marked the formative period of field work and research on dinosaurs. In a sense this exploratory phase of man's probing into the Age of Dinosaurs came to an end during the final decade of the nineteenth century, marked by the death of Cope in 1897 and of Marsh in 1899.

Then came the beginning of the modern period of dinosaur research, initiated, one might say, by the massive excavations of late Jurassic dinosaurs by the American Museum of Natural History in New York near Como Bluff, Wyoming, where Marsh had collected many specimens, and by the Carnegie Museum of Pittsburgh at what is now Dinosaur National Monument in Utah. One of the

"Professor Mudge contemplating bones" at the dinosaur quarry near Morrison, Colorado. A primitive watercolor by Arthur Lakes, who worked for Marsh.

features of the modern period of studies on dinosaurs has been the participation of large institutions having the resources of money and manpower, and a willingness to devote immense amounts of time and effort to the excavation, preparation, and study of dinosaur skeletons. It is an effort not lightly to be considered; the placing of a large dinosaur skeleton in an exhibition hall has behind it the expenditure of many man-years of labor and study. At the turn of the century, when such activities were begun, the cost of a large dinosaur skeleton was immense; today it is prodigious. It is no wonder that only a chosen few of the museums of the world have attempted programs of dinosaurian research.

In 1891 Henry Fairfield Osborn (1857–1935) came to the American Museum of Natural History from Princeton, to establish a program of field work and research on fossil vertebrates—the remains of animals with backbones. Among other considerations, Osborn was anxious to obtain some dinosaurs, not only for their scientific value, but also because skeletons of these extinct reptiles would bring attention and support to the museum. Consequently a field party from the museum, including Walter Granger, who spent his life as one of the museum's great paleontologists, and Barnum Brown, who likewise had a long career at the museum to become famous as one of the greatest of the

Another Lakes watercolor showing E. Kennedy and Bill Reed with dinosaur bones at Como Bluff, Wyoming.

A restoration of *Diplodocus* by Charles R. Knight.

dinosaur hunters, spent the summer of 1897 exploring and collecting in the Upper Jurassic Morrison Formation at Marsh's old stamping ground at Como Bluff, in the southeastern corner of Wyoming. During the following summer the search was widened, and on the Medicine Bow anticline, at a place subsequently christened Bone Cabin, dinosaur bones were found in great profusion, littering the ground. The large bones were so numerous that a sheepherder had used them to build a cabin—hence the name given to this locality. So here the museum carried on an extensive operation, lasting several years, and resulting in the acquisition of many fine dinosaurs, some of which may be seen on display in New York.

About a decade later, in 1909, Earl Douglass of

Friedrich von Huene as a young man. Huene was one of the outstanding twentieth-century authorities on dinosaurs. He lived a long, vigorous, and productive life, and was actively studying dinosaurs when he was an elderly man.

the Carnegie Museum found a promising deposit of Morrison dinosaur bones near Split Mountain, Utah, where the Green River emerges from the mountains to cross a valley east of Vernal. He began to excavate, and the more he dug, the more he found. This was the beginning of an extraordinary quarrying effort that lasted through many years and provided the Carnegie Museum with so many tons of dinosaur skeletons that they still have not been completely unpacked and prepared. The power behind this almost unprecedented quarrying operation was Andrew Carnegie, whose millions had endowed the museum. Carnegie became passionately interested in the dinosaurs that were being dug up in Utah, so much so that through the years he poured large sums of money into the project. At the end of each field season massive crates filled with dinosaur bones in rock were shipped to Pittsburgh to be added to the museum's collection, all to the great satisfaction of Mr. Carnegie.

At the same time that Douglass was developing his large quarry in Utah, another giant operation was being carried forward in sediments of the same age in what was then German East Africa, what is now Tanzania. At a locality known as Tendaguru the Berlin Museum of Natural Science excavated numerous Upper Jurassic fossils, including the skeleton of *Brachiosaurus*, at that time the largest of

all known dinosaurs. To say that this was a gigantic operation is no exaggeration; at the height of the work the German paleontologists employed some five hundred native laborers, who lived at the site with their families, thereby establishing a village of considerable size in the vicinity of the quarries. The huge bones were taken out of the ground, prepared for shipment, and carried on the backs of porters to Lindi, a seaport four days distant by trail from Tendaguru, for transport to Berlin.

In the years immediately before and during the First World War, there was a rush to collect Cretaceous dinosaurs in the badlands of the Red Deer River of southern Alberta. The principal actors in this drama were Barnum Brown of the American Museum (already mentioned), Charles Sternberg and his sons, Charles, George, and Levi, of the National Museum of Canada in Ottawa, and W. A. Parks of the Royal Ontario Museum in Toronto. There was a friendly and picturesque rivalry between the fossil hunters; they floated down the Red Deer River on large rafts, from which aquatic camps they prospected for and excavated dinosaur skeletons in the steep badland cliffs that bordered the river. As a result magnificent collections were accumulated, now to be seen in the museums in Ottawa, Toronto, and New York.

The story of the search for dinosaurs could be

expanded to fill a book. At this place only a bare outline of what has been done since the early years of the present century can be set forth. In brief, the search and its resultant research has continued, and has reached out to all parts of the world. As a consequence the numbers and variety of known dinosaurs have grown enormously since the end of the First World War, and especially during the past few decades. In spite of the great expense certain museums have continued or have inaugurated programs on dinosaurs. Such work has in a way been facilitated by the development of modern technology, making the procurement of large fossils in the field and the handling of these materials in the laboratory more practical than formerly had been the case. Powerful trucks and winches and mechanical hammers and chisels in the field, air hammers and abrasive equipment in the laboratory, have eased the problem of dealing with large, heavy fossils. And the ever-growing interest in dinosaurs, not only among the scientists who are continually learning new facts about these extinct reptiles, but among the public, for whom the story of dinosaurian evolution is becoming increasingly popular, has stimulated the never-ending fossil hunt.

In North America recent work on dinosaurs has been largely concerned with the early, primitive dinosaurs of Triassic age and the advanced, highly varied dinosaurs of the Cretaceous. Less attention has been devoted to the Jurassic dinosaurs, perhaps because they are frequently of gigantic size and therefore difficult and expensive to collect, prepare, and study. Mention should be made, however, of the work carried forward by James Jensen of Brigham Young University, in Utah, where, among other things, he has collected the bones of an immense dinosaur of late Jurassic age, notably larger than the huge *Brachiosaurus* discovered by the Germans at Tendaguru.

As for Triassic dinosaurs, a remarkable concentration of skeletons of the little carnivorous dinosaur *Coelophysis* was discovered at Ghost Ranch in northwestern New Mexico some thirty-five years ago, affording detailed knowledge as to the anatomy of this early representative of its order. To say that the concentration of fossils at this locality was remarkable does not in any way overstate the fact. Dozens of skeletons representing dinosaurs of all ages, from very young individuals to full adults, were found piled up in an almost inextricable mass, necks and bodies, legs and tails intertwined to form a picture of unusual confusion. A large quarry was excavated in order to expose and remove the fossils, of which some are among the most completely known articulated dinosaur skeletons. In recent years the quarry has been reopened and further excavated, yielding

WHAT IS A DINOSAUR?

It is ironic that Richard Owen's definition of the Dinosauria, the original basis for the recognition of these long-extinct reptiles, does not in the light of modern knowledge adequately describe the salient characters that make the dinosaurs what they are (or were). The sentence from Owen's paper of 1841 (published in 1842) establishing the name *Dinosauria* was quoted above on page 17. But let us look in a little more detail at Owen's original definition of the dinosaurs. It comes from a rather rare volume, and is worth repeating at this place.

Late Jurassic life in North America as revealed by the fossils of the Morrison Formation. In the left foreground is the giant carnosaur *Allosaurus,* in the right foreground is the small coelurosaur *Ornitholestes.* Behind *Ornitholestes* is the plated ornithischian *Stegosaurus.* In the background are seen the sauropods *Apatosaurus.* A turtle also is evident in the picture. As contrasted with the Triassic scene (page 54) dinosaurs dominate the land. The plants are primitive—cycads and conifers being abundant. The climate obviously was tropical.

A late Cretaceous scene in western North America, based upon fossils found in the Oldman Formation of Alberta. In the left foreground is the giant carnosaur *Albertosaurus,* in the right foreground and background are the crested hadrosaurs *Corythosaurus.* Behind and between them is the armored ornithischian *Ankylosaurus,* while in the background at the left are two individuals of the horned dinosaur *Styracosaurus.* The vegetation has taken on a modern appearance with various deciduous angiosperms abundant. The climate was probably subtropical.

This group, which includes at least three well-established genera [*Iguanodon* and *Hylaeosaurus* described by Mantell, and *Megalosaurus* described by Buckland] of Saurians [reptiles], is characterized by a large sacrum [connection of backbone with pelvis] composed of five anchylosed [coalesced] vertebrae of unusual construction, by the height and breadth and outward sculpturing of the neural arch [protecting the spinal nerve] of the dorsal [back] vertebrae, by the twofold articulation [joining] of the ribs to the vertebrae, viz. at the anterior part of the spine [of each vertebra] by a head and tubercle, and along the rest of the trunk by a turbercle attached to the transverse process [of each vertebra] only; by broad and sometimes complicated coracoids and long and slender clavicles [bones in shoulder girdle], whereby Crocodilian characters of the vertebral column are combined with a Lacertilian [lizard] type of the pectoral arch [or shoulder girdle]; the dental organs [teeth] also exhibit the same transitional or annectent characters in a greater or less degree. The bones of the extremities are of large proportional size, for Saurians; they are provided with large medullary [marrow] cavities, and with well-developed and unusual processes, and are terminated by metacarpal [long bones of the hand], metatarsal [and of foot] and phalangeal [finger and toe] bones, which, with the exception of the ungual phalanges [claws or hooves], more or less resemble those of the heavy pachydermal Mammals, and attest, with the hollow long-bones, the terrestrial habits of the species. (Richard Owen, *Report on British Fossil Reptiles* [British Association for the Advancement of Science, 1842], pages 102–103.)

And in the succeeuing paragraph, already quoted, he goes on to justify his establishment of the name *Dinosauria*.

The sacrum, composed of five vertebrae, that Owen cites at the beginning of his definition, is common among the dinosaurs, but not always of this particular number. Some dinosaurs may have fewer, some more vertebrae in the sacrum. The characters of the dorsal vertebrae and the articulations of the ribs are certainly typical of the dinosaurs, but are found in some related reptiles as well, such as crocodiles. The dinosaurs do have broad coracoid bones, but clavicles are not characteristic among these reptiles. What Owen means by "annectent" dental characters it is hard to say; dinosaurs show great variety in the dentition. He is correct in emphasizing the large hollow limb bones (although in some of the gigantic dinosaurs the limb bones are very solid) and he is correct in recognizing the "terrestrial habits of the species." All of the dinosaurs were terrestrial reptiles, although some of them were of amphibious habits. Finally, not all dinosaurs were of great size, and it is evident that they do not represent "a distinct tribe" as Owen states in the sentence whereby he established the name, but rather two very distinct reptilian orders.

It is easy, of course, to criticize from the vantage point of hindsight, so one need not fault Owen for his imperfect definition of the dinosaurs. He was, after all, basing his concept on three imperfectly known genera. The important fact is that Owen *did* recognize these fossil reptiles for what they were, as land-living animals very different from any modern reptiles.

How, then, are we to recognize the dinosaurs?

They are defined by certain anatomical characters, as preserved in their skeletons. They are not to be defined by size, for as has been mentioned all of them are not large; indeed some dinosaurs are no larger than small chickens. In this respect, perhaps we may compare our recognition of the long-extinct dinosaurs with our recognition of modern animals, say of the cats. Cats, in the large sense of the word, come in all sizes, from the awesome Siberian tiger to the gentle house cat. They come in a variety of color patterns: stripes, spots, marbled patterns, and solid colors. Yet we immediately know them as cats—by the shape of the head, by the teeth, by the supple bodies and the padded feet. The common features of their anatomy unite them into a coherent group.

The basic feature for the definition of the dinosaurs is the structure of the pelvis. There are two types of dinosaurian pelvis, a fact that was established by the English paleontologist H. G. Seeley, in 1887. One pelvic type is characterized by a triradiate arrangement of the three pelvic bones, ilium, pubis and ischium, when the structure is viewed from the side. In such a pelvis the elongated ilium, which connects the pelvis with the sacral vertebrae of the backbone, surmounts two downwardly directed, rather rod-like or plate-like bones, the pubis projecting forwardly and the ischium projecting to the rear, an arrangement seen in modern reptiles. Where the three bones are joined there is a large, rounded opening, the acetabulum, for articulation

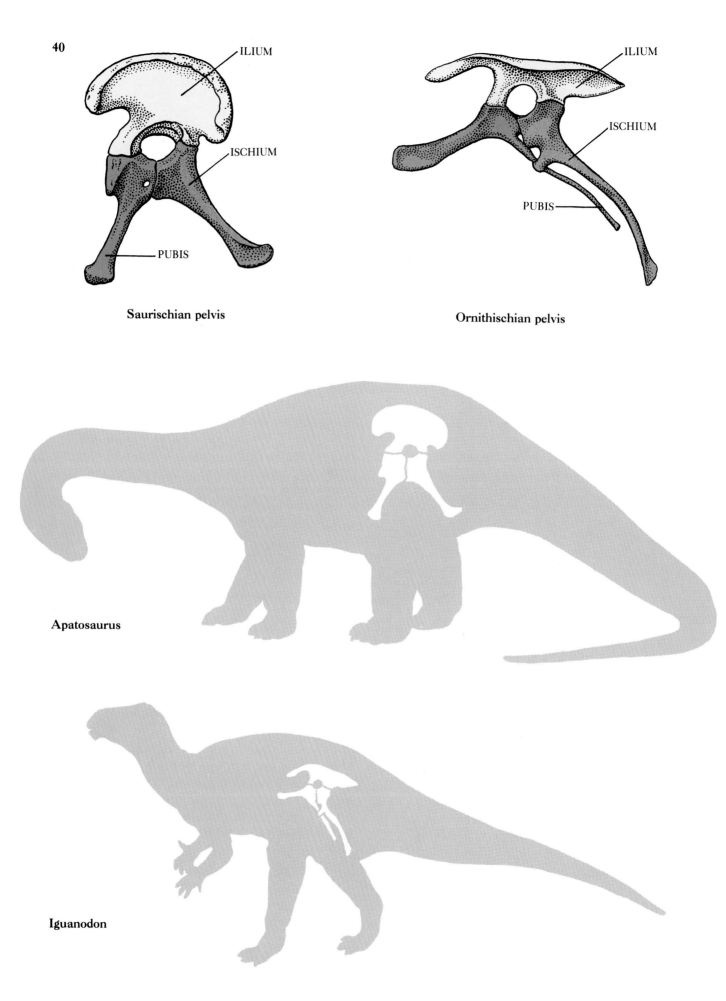

40

ILIUM

ISCHIUM

PUBIS

Saurischian pelvis

ILIUM

ISCHIUM

PUBIS

Ornithischian pelvis

Apatosaurus

Iguanodon

with the upper end of the femur. Such a pelvis is characteristic of the *Saurischia*, one of the two dinosaurian orders. The other pelvic type is characterized by the fact that the pubis has rotated to the rear, to lie adjacent and parallel to the ischium, an arrangement that is somewhat similar to the relationship of pubis and ischium in the birds. Very frequently, among the dinosaurs typified by this form of pelvis, there is a strong forward process, or projection, on the pubis, and this prepubis, together with the backwardly projecting combined pubis and ischium, as well as anterior and posterior processes on the ilium, gives the pelvis a quadriradiate structure. Such a pelvis is characteristic of the *Ornithischia*, the other of the two dinosaurian orders.

There are, of course, other anatomical characters that go along with the two types of pelvis to distinguish the two orders of dinosaurs.

In addition to the distinctive "reptile-hip," triradiate pelvis, saurischians are characterized by having teeth generally present throughout the length of the jaws (although in some saurischians teeth are more or less restricted to the fronts of the jaws), and the teeth are of simple form. The toes, when complete, terminate in claws. The saurischians show a subdivision into carnivorous and herbivorous forms.

The ornithischian dinosaurs, with the "bird-hip," tetraradiate pelvis, generally have teeth only on the sides of the jaws, the toothless fronts of the jaws being modified into a sort of beak. The teeth are often of complex form, and may be extraordinarily numerous. The toes frequently terminate in hooves, rather than in claws. The ornithischians were entirely herbivorous throughout the extent of their evolutionary history.

The two orders of dinosaurs have been internally classified in various ways, but for our purposes the Saurischia may be divided into three suborders: the Theropoda, these being carnivorous and the only dinosaurs to be meat-eaters; the Sauropoda, the gigantic brontosaurs and their relatives; and the Prosauropoda, Triassic dinosaurs more or less intermediate between the theropods and sauropods, and if not directly ancestral to the sauropods certainly closely related in origins to the great giants. The Ornithischia may be divided into four suborders: the Ornithopoda, including the duck-billed dinosaurs and their relatives; the Stegosauria, or plated dinosaurs; the Ankylosauria, or armored dinosaurs; and the Ceratospsia, or horned dinosaurs.

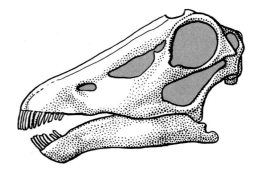

Saurischian skull and jaw. *Apatosaurus.*

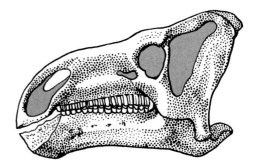

Ornithischian skull and jaw. *Iguanodon.*

CRETACEOUS

Ceratopsians

Ankylosaurs

JURASSIC

Ornithopods

Stegosaurs

Theropods

Sauropods

Ornithischians

UPPER
TRIASSIC

Saurischians

Prosauropods

Evolution of the two orders of dinosaurs, the several suborders being represented in each case by a characteristic genus. As the dinosaurs evolved so also did the environments in which they lived—from primitive Triassic and Jurassic gymnosperm jungles to Cretaceous angiosperm woodlands of modern aspect.

In summary the primary classification of the two orders of dinosaurs may be set down in tabular form as follows:

Order	Suborder	Order	Suborder
Saurischia	Theropoda Prosauropoda Sauropoda	Ornithischia	Ornithopoda Stegosauria Ankylosauria Ceratopsia

Within this rather formal arrangement of the saurischian and ornithischian dinosaurs various subdivisions have been recognized—not always the same by different authorities. For our purposes it will be convenient to distinguish about a dozen groups of dinosaurs, some of subordinal rank, some of lesser consequence, each group showing its own adaptations for its own manner of living. Of course each dinosaurian group herewith identified is composed of related genera and species; in some cases a great many, in others only a few. Whether numerous or restricted, the dinosaurs contained within a single group show similar and related specializations.

Among the saurischian dinosaurs the theropods may be divided into:

1. **coelurosaurs,** or the small carnivores, and
2. **carnosaurs,** or the medium to large and even gigantic carnivores.

The coelurosaurs (1), typified by the Triassic genus *Coelophysis,* are generally among the smallest of

Coelophysis (1)

Tyrannosaurus (2)

the dinosaurs; some are no larger than chickens, others may be as large as ostriches. The comparison with birds is apt, because these dinosaurs are very bird-like in many respects. (It might be more correct to say that birds are much like these particular dinosaurs, for there is good reason to think that the birds are in fact descended from coelurosaurian dinosaurs.) The skeleton is very lightly built, with hollow bones. The body is pivoted at the hips, so that the coelurosaurs walked and ran on hind limbs that are remarkably similar to the legs of birds—so similar indeed that the trackways of early coelurosaurian dinosaurs found in Connecticut were, as we have seen, mistaken for the footprints of birds. The forelimbs in these dinosaurs are small, and were never used for locomotion. They terminate in hands armed with sharp claws that would have been useful for catching prey or digging for food. The tail

is long, and in life served to counterbalance the weight of the body, while the neck, too, is long and supple. At the end of this neck is a small rather delicate skull, the jaws of which contain many sharp teeth, nicely adapted for catching and tearing food. In some of the later coelurosaurs, the struthiomimids, or "ostrich dinosaurs," as typified by *Struthiomimus*, the jaws are completely without teeth, and take the form of a bird-like bill.

The carnosaurs (2), of which the well-known dinosaur *Tyrannosaurus* is a highly evolved example, show a strong trend toward gigantic size. Yet even though these dinosaurs became large and even gigantic, they retain the primary adaptations of their coelurosaurian ancestors. They walked on strong hind limbs, the fore limbs are small, and the tail is a long counterbalance. But among the carnosaurs the skull is very large—often inordinately so, in order to provide long jaws and huge teeth for the killing of large victims. And since the skull is large, the neck is relatively short; it would have been quite disadvantageous to try to carry such a large skull on a long, flexible neck.

This brings us to:

3. **prosauropods,** the proto-giants.

These dinosaurs, unlike any other dinosaurs, are mainly confined to the Triassic Period, a time of dinosaur beginnings. Although most of the Triassic dinosaurs are small, as might be expected of ancestral forms, the prosauropods (3), as typified by *Plateosaurus*, are of considerable size, commonly being twenty feet or more in length. They show many of the ancestral saurischian features, such as bipedalism, a long neck, and a long tail. But the prosauropods also show departures from a primitive pattern; the hind limbs and feet are heavy (for the support of weight) and the fore limbs are secondarily enlarged, so that this dinosaur might have walked about as easily in a four-footed pose as in the more atavistic bipedal fashion. The teeth in the small skull are no longer sharp blades; rather they take the form of somewhat expanded leaf-like structures, with little crenulations along their edges, all set very close together. Such a dental system is obviously adapted for the cropping of plant food.

Whether the prosauropods are direct ancestors or not, they are obviously prophetic of the:

4. **sauropods,** the greatest of the giants.

Apatosaurus, more commonly known as *Brontosaurus*,* is typical of the sauropods (4), and is perhaps the stereotype that most people have in mind when the word *dinosaur* is mentioned. The sauropods are the largest of the dinosaurs, reaching lengths of seventy-five feet and more, and probable live weights of as much as forty tons, even up to eighty tons in the case of the immense *Brachiosaurus*. Because of their tremendous size these dino-

---

*Although *Apatosaurus* is the correct name, *Brontosaurus*, being well established in the literature, is widely used. The term brontosaur may be applied to sauropods of this type.

Plateosaurus (3)

Apatosaurus (4)

saurs were permanently quadrupedal, so the fore limbs are large, yet in most cases not so large as the hind limbs. The limb bones are solid; the feet are short and broad, obviously provided in life with heavy pads like the feet of elephants (as is shown by fossil footprints) to support the great weight of the body and to take up the shocks of enormously heavy strides. In these dinosaurs the neck and the tail are very long, and the vertebrae are remarkably constructed to be relatively light yet very strong. These vertebrae are built something in the manner of open steelwork, so that bone is present along lines of force while otherwise there are great open spaces. There are extra articulations to provide strength between individual vertebrae, and along the neck the spines of the vertebrae are divided to form in each case a large V, with its open end at the top. The succession of such V-shaped spines provides a long trough along the back, within which was housed during life a long, strong ligament, the *ligamentum nuchae*, that acted like the cable on a derrick. The skull, although large when held in the arms of an enquiring scientist, is relatively very small; the jaws are weak; and teeth, relatively few in number, are restricted to the fronts of the jaws.

Such are the four adaptational types of saurischian dinosaurs. The ornithischian dinosaurs, far more varied than the saurischians, may now be considered.

Among the ornithischians the most varied suborder, that of the ornithopods, may be divided into:

5. **hypsilophodonts,** a mixed lot of primitive herbivores,

6. **iguanodonts,** which may also be called camptosaurs,

7. **pachycephalosaurs,** or dome-headed dinosaurs, and

8. **hadrosaurs,** or duck-billed dinosaurs.

The hypsilophodonts (5), the most primitive of the ornithopod dinosaurs, appear in the Upper Triassic beds of South Africa, where they are known from the skeletons of *Heterodontosaurus* and *Lesothosaurus*, and in sediments of about the same age in North America, which have yielded the skeleton of *Scutellosaurus.** *Hypsilophodon* itself, which is of Cretaceous age and is found in Europe, is none the less of primitive form, retaining many of the characters that typify the ancestral saurischian dinosaurs. All of these dinosaurs are small and all are bipedal, although it is obvious that generally they had the capacity to walk on all four feet. This was a

*The Kayenta Formation of Arizona, in which *Scutellosaurus* is found, is considered either as of Upper Triassic or Lower Jurassic affinities (see page 70). *Scutellosaurus* is discussed with early ornithischians of late Triassic age (see pages 71 and 72).

trend quite characteristic of the ornithopod dinosaurs. Perhaps the most significant feature of the hypsilophodonts is the dentition, which even in the most primitive of the Triassic genera is already strongly adapted for the eating of plant food. Such teeth, present only in the sides of the jaws, are triangular in shape, compressed from side to side, and have along their front and back edges a series of crenulations or cusplets, like the edges of a serrated leaf. From teeth like this, which are relatively simple, there evolved the highly specialized teeth, coordinated into complex dental batteries, so well de-

A saurischian dinosaur, the gigantic Jurassic sauropod *Apatosaurus* as depicted by Charles R. Knight in 1897.

An ornithischian dinosaur, the Cretaceous duck-billed dinosaur *Anatosaurus*, painted by Charles R. Knight in 1909.

veloped in many of the advanced ornithischian dinosaurs. The fronts of the jaws lack teeth, and form in the ornithopods, as well as in other ornithischians, a bird-like beak that in life obviously had a horny covering. *Scutellosaurus* is amply provided with protective armor plate, the harbinger of a development that was to typify some other ornithischian dinosaurs.

From ancestors showing the characters that have been described above, the later ornithopods evolved along three diverging lines. One was that of the camptosaurs (6), which are generalized and characterized by low skulls with broad beaks. *Iguanodon*, the dinosaur that was discovered by Mrs. Mantell and described by Gideon Mantell, is the largest and most advanced among this group—a gigantic browsing herbivore with strong limbs and with a sharp spike on the thumb.

The dome-headed dinosaurs (7), some quite small, others of gigantic size, are in most respects like other ornithopods, but are noteworthy because the top of the skull is thickened into a massive, bulbous dome, seemingly used for butting, somewhat in the way that modern rams collide head-on in their fights for dominance.

The most varied and spectacular of the ornitho-

Lesothosaurus (5)

Iguanodon (6)

49

pods are the hadrosaurs (8), in which the front of the elongated skull and jaws are broadened into a large flattened beak, remarkably like a gigantic duck's bill. Variety within the hadrosaurs is provided by the development of bony crests on the top of the skull, these crests showing a remarkable range of sizes and shapes. In many of the duck-billed dinosaurs the crests are hollow, and in life housed loops of the nasal passage. The significance of such developments will be explored on subsequent pag-

es. Among the hardrosaurs the teeth are evolved beyond anything seen in other dinosaurs; these reptiles have very complex dental batteries containing numerous rows of teeth, often with as many as several hundred teeth in each jaw. This system of tooth development, much too intricate to be considered here, will be described later.

In contrast to the rich development of the ornithopod dinosaurs is the restricted suborder known as the:

Pachycephalosaurus (7)

Corythosaurus (8)

Stegosaurus (9)

Ankylosaurus (10)

Psittacosaurus (11)

9. **stegosaurs,** or plated dinosaurs.

These ornithischians are represented by only a few genera, yet as typified by *Stegosaurus* (9), they are among the most bizarre of the dinosaurs. They are large, quadrupedal reptiles with strong limbs. In *Stegosaurus* the fore limbs are remarkably short as compared with the hind limbs, so that the back arches up to a high point at the hips. The skull is very small, the beaked jaws are weak, and the teeth are limited. But the most striking feature of *Stegosaurus* is the double row of immense, triangular plates rising along the length of the back, while at the end of the tail there is a complement of four long and fearsome spikes.

Closely related to the stegosaurs are the:

10. **ankylosaurs,** or armored dinosaurs.

These large, squat ornithischians, among which *Ankylosaurus* (10) is typical, are protected by bony armor plates that in life were covered with horny skin. The protection is extensive, covering the back and sides, much of the limbs, and the skull. In some ankylosaurs such as *Ankylosaurus*, the tail ends in a massive, bony club, a sort of flail that in life must have been used to great effect. The teeth of these dinosaurs are very weak; the ankylosaurs must have subsisted upon soft vegetation.

One small group of the ornithischian dinosaurs, commonly included within the ornithopods but here listed separately and represented by a single genus, may be called:

11. **psittacosaurs,** or parrot-beaked dinosaurs.

Psittacosaurus (11), known from Mongolia, is a small ornithischian, in most respects a typical ornithopod. But in this dinosaur the skull is deep and narrow, and in front is compressed into a parrot-like beak. There is good reason to think that *Psittacosaurus*, of Cretaceous age, may have been ancestral to the horned dinosaurs.

The last of the dinosaurs, arising and evolving during late Cretaceous time are the:

12. **ceratopsians,** or horned dinosaurs.

These are for the most part very large, quadrupedal ornithischian dinosaurs, noteworthy because of the huge size of the skull. The back of the skull is expanded into a great bony frill, extending back over the shoulders. *Triceratops* (12), perhaps the best-known genus, has two long brow horns, one over each eye, and a smaller horn on the nose. As in other ceratopsians the front of the skull is compressed into a deep, very sharp beak, evidently derived from a *Psittacosaurus*-like ancestor. The ceratopsians rival the hadrosaurs in variety; in this case such variety is achieved by the different form of the frill in the various genera, and by the different development of the horns, some long, some short. *Protoceratops*, a small ceratopsian from Mongolia, admirably fulfills the role of ancestor to the giant horned dinosaurs, and provides a connecting link between them and an ancestor such as *Psittacosaurus*.

It is quite clear from the fossil record that the two orders of dinosaurs were distinct from their very beginnings in middle and late Triassic time. Even the earliest representatives of the two orders show the salient characters of pelvis, limbs and feet, skull, and teeth that differentiate them throughout their long, separate evolutionary histories. Yet it would seem that eventually they had a common ancestry, perhaps during the early years of the Triassic Period. That ancestry was within a group of Triassic reptiles known as thecodonts—reptiles that had arisen during the transition from Permian to Triassic time (the Permian Period being the geological period immediately preceding the Triassic).

During long ages of geologic history before the advent of the Triassic Period the reptiles had gone through their primary evolutionary radiation, progressing in several directions from primitive ancestors, in turn derived from amphibian forebears. One of the features of early reptilian evolution was the appearance and the wide deployment of the synapsids, or mammal-like reptiles, those reptiles developing along lines that within certain groups were to give rise directly to the first mammals. The mammal-like reptiles truly dominated Permian landscapes, and it would seem as if they were destined to continue indefinitely along their several evolutionary lines.

But with the beginning of the Triassic Period the thecodont reptiles had appeared on the scene, to evolve rapidly in many directions, thereby crowding the mammal-like reptiles out of their position of dominance. By the end of Triassic time the mam-

Triceratops (12)

M. COLBERT

A late Triassic scene in what is now the American Southwest, showing animals and plants represented by fossils in the Chinle Formation. In the left foreground is the large labyrinthodont amphibian *Metoposaurus,* in the right foreground is the giant thecodont phytosaur *Rutiodon.* Behind the amphibian is a small thecodont *Hesperosuchus,* while behind the phytosaur is the large armored thecodont *Desmatosuchus.* In the background, left, are the only dinosaurs in this scene, the early saurischian *Coelophysis.* Large scouring rushes or horsetails, cycads, and ferns cover the ground, while araucarian pines reach into the sky. At that time southwestern North America was a tropical land near sea level, and much closer to the equator than it is today.

54

mal-like reptiles had become almost extinct, but before they had disappeared from the face of the earth one branch of this numerous and varied assemblage gave rise to the first Triassic mammals. One might think that from this point the mammals would have evolved rapidly to supplant the reptiles as the dominant land animals, but such was not to be the case. The first Triassic mammals were very small, unobtrusive creatures, and so they continued through the remainder of Mesozoic time. There were, within these tiny animals, great potentials for evolutionary advancement, but so long as the thecodonts and their dinosaurian descendants occupied the continents in great variety and profusion, the mammals were held to a very secondary role in the pattern of life.

Within the thecodonts there had been established a series of adaptations that gave them distinct advantages over their mammal-like reptile and mammal contemporaries. Among these adaptations were a lightly constructed but strong skull with long jaws, a skeleton in which the bones likewise were lightly constructed but strong (in contrast to the rather "clumsy" skeleton of many mammal-like reptiles), and a posture whereby the limbs were brought well beneath the body to keep it raised off the ground. Thus the thecodonts were fast-moving, aggressive reptiles, and they prevailed.

From the thecodonts there arose during Triassic time the two orders of dinosaurs, the crocodiles, and the pterosaurs, or flying reptiles. All of these reptiles—thecodonts, saurischians, ornithischians, crocodiles, and pterosaurs—are known as archosaurs, and the Mesozoic Era, consisting of the

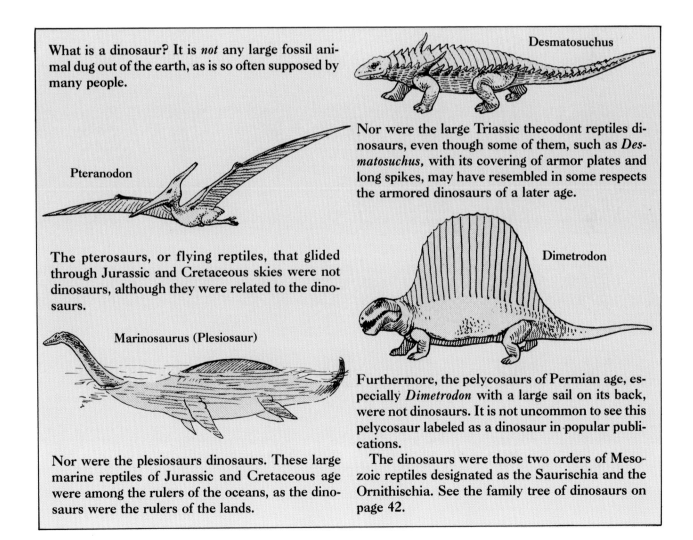

What is a dinosaur? It is *not* any large fossil animal dug out of the earth, as is so often supposed by many people.

Pteranodon

The pterosaurs, or flying reptiles, that glided through Jurassic and Cretaceous skies were not dinosaurs, although they were related to the dinosaurs.

Marinosaurus (Plesiosaur)

Nor were the plesiosaurs dinosaurs. These large marine reptiles of Jurassic and Cretaceous age were among the rulers of the oceans, as the dinosaurs were the rulers of the lands.

Desmatosuchus

Nor were the large Triassic thecodont reptiles dinosaurs, even though some of them, such as *Desmatosuchus*, with its covering of armor plates and long spikes, may have resembled in some respects the armored dinosaurs of a later age.

Dimetrodon

Furthermore, the pelycosaurs of Permian age, especially *Dimetrodon* with a large sail on its back, were not dinosaurs. It is not uncommon to see this pelycosaur labeled as a dinosaur in popular publications.

The dinosaurs were those two orders of Mesozoic reptiles designated as the Saurischia and the Ornithischia. See the family tree of dinosaurs on page 42.

ERA	DURATION (millions of years)	PERIOD	DURATION (millions of years)	MILLIONS OF YEARS AGO	EVOLUTION OF LIFE AS RECORDED BY FOSSILS
CENOZOIC	65	Quaternary	3	3	Origin and evolution of man
		Tertiary	62		Evolution of mammals
MESOZOIC	160	Cretaceous	70	65	Extinction of dinosaurs
					Zenith of dinosaurs
					Bony fishes
					Flowering plants
		Jurassic	55	135	First birds
					Development of giant dinosaurs
		Triassic	35	190	First dinosaurs
					First mammals
				225	Wide extinctions
PALEOZOIC	345	Permian	50		Dominance of mammal-like reptiles
		(Pennsylvanian) Carboniferous (Mississippian)	70	275	First reptiles
					Dominance of amphibians
		Devonian	55	345	First amphibians
					Air-breathing fishes
					Primitive land plants
		Silurian	30	400	First jawed fishes
					First land-living animals
		Ordovician	70	430	Jawless fishes
		Cambrian	70	500	First vertebrates
					Invertebrates widely established
					Appearance of numerous fossils
		"Precambrian"	4000	570	Fossils rare
					Algae
					Origin of Earth

The scale of geologic time has been developed through more than a century and a half of research in field and laboratory. It is accepted throughout the world, as shown in this chart, so that geologists and paleontologists have a common ground for discussions of time and fossils.

The rocks of the earth are divided into a sequence of *systems* and the time during which any system of rocks was deposited is called a *period*. Periods are grouped into larger time divisions known as *eras,* and they may be divided into smaller units known as *epochs*.

Subdivisions of rocks within any particular system are generally designated as lower, middle, and upper. Thus Upper Triassic rocks contain early dinosaurs. Subdivisions of periods or epochs in terms of time are designated as early, middle, and late. Thus early dinosaurs lived during late Triassic time.

The earth is on the order of four and a half billion years of age. For much of this immense span of time there is no fossil record; only during the past six hundred million years do we have an adequate representation of life on the earth as revealed by fossils. Life was certainly present much earlier than six hundred million years ago, but it is probable that such life was in the form of small, primitive organisms without hard parts, which thus were not fossilized. Furthermore, the complex dynamics of earth movements during earlier eras probably destroyed most of the ancient organisms preserved as fossils. Nevertheless some traces of very ancient life have been found in rocks of great age.

The fossil record begins, for all practical purposes, in early Cambrian rocks, and can be traced in ever increasing complexity from then until modern times. (Such fossils as are found in rocks earlier than Cambrian age are commonly referred to as *Precambrian* in age.)

Dinosaurs arose during late Triassic time, about two hundred million years ago. They lived through a span of about one hundred forty million years, becoming extinct about sixty-five million years ago.

An absolute scale of geologic time has been established during the past few decades by the study of radioactive elements, included in some rocks when they were formed. These elements have decayed, and knowing the rate of decay, the proportions of a radioactive element to its end product in any particular rock will determine its age. Thus the transformation of uranium into lead is accomplished by the discharge of alpha particles, and the rate of this discharge can be measured by the use of a Geiger counter. By determining the proportions of uranium and lead in the rock, and knowing the rate of discharge of alpha particles, the age of rock may be calculated. Other methods rely on measurements of the ratios of potassium to argon, or of rubidium to strontium in certain rocks. Checks and cross-checks have demonstrated the validity of these studies.

Therefore we can speak today of the geologic age of the various dinosaurs with a high degree of confidence—as contrasted with former years, when such age determinations were at best based upon educated guesses.

Triassic, Jurassic, and Cretaceous periods, was the age of archosaurs. Archosaurs were ubiquitous on the Mesozoic continents; and supreme over all were the two orders of dinosaurs. (The birds, arising during the Jurassic Period, are derived from archosaurs, perhaps descended from thecodont ancestors, perhaps from saurischian dinosaurs.)

It was mentioned above that the thecodonts are typified by a lightly constructed, strong skull with long jaws. Such a skull is characteristic of all of the archosaurs, and a few additional words concerning it may be helpful at this place.

The archosaur skull, in its original state, was rather narrow and deep, and when looked at from various angles is notable for its open construction. On each side of the skull is the orbit, the opening that contained the eye, and at the very front the naris, the opening for the nostril. Between the naris and the eye is another large opening, the preorbital fenestra, which perhaps in life housed a gland, possibly a salt-excreting gland. Behind the eye are two large openings, the superior and lateral postorbital or temporal fenestrae, one piercing the skull roof, the other on the side of the skull. These openings allowed for the bulging of powerful jaw muscles. Lodged beneath the upper postorbital openings and between the lateral openings is the braincase, a relatively small, bony box.

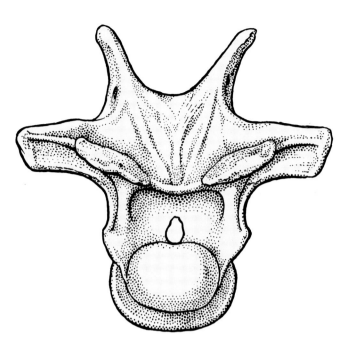

The tooth of *Scutellosaurus* has a rather complex crown (for a reptile) with small crenulations or cusplets along its edges. Such a tooth was adapted for cutting plant fibers.

The vertebra of *Apatosaurus* shows the U-shaped bifurcation of the spine to house a massive ligament that supported the long neck.

There is a large mandibular fenestra in the side of the lower jaw.

Thus the archosaurian skull and lower jaw are constructed in such a way that bone was present where needed, to surround large open spaces. It made for strength and lightness, somewhat on the principle of steel trusswork in a bridge or a roof. During the evolution of the archosaurs, notably in some of the ornithischian dinosaurs and the crocodiles, there was a trend toward secondary closing in the ancestral open skull, but it was in the beginning the open structure of the skull that contributed to the evolutionary success of the archosaurs in competition with other reptiles.

It was also the construction of the skeleton behind the skull that made the archosaurs such successful reptiles. There was a strong trend toward hollow long bones, built on the principle of a cylinder. Again, such bones are strong but light.

And finally, as has already been mentioned, the typical archosaurian posture, with the limbs brought well beneath the body, gave to these reptiles the advantage of agility not possessed by contemporary reptiles. The lines of gravitational force passed through or near the limbs, so that the archosaur was cooperating with gravity instead of fight-

ing it, as was the case with reptiles having "sprawling" limbs.

So the archosaurs, particularly the dinosaurs, became the rulers of Mesozoic times.

Perhaps something should be said about geologic time at this place, in order to give perspective to the place of the dinosaurs in earth history. Modern research, based to a considerable extent upon the study of radioactive elements, indicates that the earth is about four and a half billion years old. The first indications of life on earth have been found in Africa, in rocks that are dated at about three and a half billion years of age, these indications being microscopic rod-like objects that look like bacteria and algae. In Australia, in rocks dated at about seven hundred million years of age, there have been found the oldest evidence for multicellular organisms in the form of impressions of jellyfish and worm-like animals. But it is not until we encounter rocks dated at about six hundred million years of age that we find a well-preserved fossil record. Here, at the beginning of Cambrian time (see chart) are the fossilized remains of organisms with hard parts—trilobites, shelled brachiopods, and other animals that lived in the sea.

By the end of the Cambrian Period there appeared the first primitive fish-like animals. Fishes prospered during the early part of the Paleozoic Era; by the end of the Devonian Period, about three hundred fifty million years ago, the early amphibians derived from fish ancestors came out on the land. From the amphibians the reptiles arose during Pennsylvania time, perhaps three hundred million years ago, and from the first reptiles the primary reptilian radiation of Pennsylvanian and Permian times took place, dominated by the wide development of the mammal-like reptiles, as mentioned above.

The thecodonts, ancestors of the dinosaurs, arose during the transition from Permian to Triassic time, about two hundred thirty million years ago, but the dinosaurs did not appear until perhaps two hundred million years ago, at about the beginning of late Triassic time. Dinosaurian dominance, quickly established, lasted for something more than one hundred thirty million years, until the end of Cretaceous history, about sixty-five million years ago, at which time the dinosaurs became extinct. Since then the world has belonged to animals that evolved largely after the disappearance of the dinosaurs, particularly the mammals, the birds, the bony fishes, and of course the innumerable insects that surround us. Man, who now rules the earth, has been around for a mere two or three million years.

These are the bare bones of a story that will be told in more detail on the pages that follow. There are many dinosaurs with which we will become acquainted, and there are many aspects in the lives of these dinosaurs that we will try to interpret and understand. All in all the story of the dinosaurs is one of the great epics of life on the earth.

THE FIRST DINOSAURS

A scene in southern Germany during late Triassic time. Although many of the early dinosaurs were quite small, as exemplified by *Procompsognathus* in the foreground, the trend toward gigantic size, so common in the dinosaurs, had already begun. The prosauropod *Plateosaurus,* dominating this scene, had attained a length of twenty feet. Concomitant with large size and a heavy body are strong limbs for proper support. *Plateosaurus* retained its ancestral bipedal posture but alternatively it probably adopted a quadrupedal pose on many occasions—a manner of walking that would have been comfortable for such a heavy reptile.

Of the thousands of fossil footprints discovered by Edward Hitchcock in the Connecticut Valley during the early and middle years of the nineteenth century, there are many that he thought had been made by ancient birds. Subsequently it was realized that the Connecticut Valley footprints are for the most part the records of early dinosaurs wandering across an ancient landscape, dinosaurs that can be recognized as Triassic theropods, prosauropods, and ornithopods. The footprints that looked so very much like the tracks of birds are those of coelurosaurians.

How can the trackways made by animals that lived two hundred million years ago be related to the animals? It is not easy. If there are skeletal remains contemporaneous with the footprints it is often possible to match bony feet and muddy tracks, now turned to stone, in a general way. But footprints can be variously deceptive; the same animal will make different-looking trackways, depending on whether it is standing, walking, or running,

One of the earliest dinosaurs was *Coelophysis,* a coelurosaur about six feet in length, found in the Upper Triassic
Chinle Formation of southwestern North America.
Even though *Coelophysis* was a primitive dinosaur it was
nevertheless a highly specialized reptile. Lightly built
and agile, it could run with considerable speed on its
bird-like hind limbs. The small fore limbs, each with
three supple fingers, obviously were used as aids in
catching small reptiles, insects, and other prey. Here we
see a basic dinosaurian structural pattern, as yet with
few indications of the gigantesque features that were to
characterize so many of the later dinosaurs.

whether the ground is wet or dry, sandy or muddy, whether at the time it was raining or the wind was blowing, whether the animal was moving on a level surface or going uphill or downhill. Finally, to add to the complications, footprints and bones rarely are preserved together. The conditions favorable for the preservation of footprints evidently were not favorable for the preservation of bones, and vice versa. So the interpretation of fossil footprints is an art in itself, to which not many scientists have devoted their attention.

In spite of such difficulties some of the Connecticut Valley footprints have been correlated with certain dinosaurs known from their bony remains. One such dinosaur is *Coelophysis*, from the Upper Triassic Chinle Formation of New Mexico. Scattered bones of this dinosaur were found in 1881 and described by Edward Drinker Cope, whom we met in the first chapter. There was then a long hiatus in time—until 1947, when, as we have seen, a party from the American Museum of Natural History in New York unearthed a fabulous concentration of *Coelophysis* skeletons at Ghost Ranch in northern New Mexico. The *Coelophysis* quarry, which was worked in 1947 and 1948, and again in recent years, has yielded skeletons of almost all ages, from very young individuals to adults, so that this is one of the most completely documented of the dinosaurs.

Footprints of Triassic dinosaurs on a rock surface at Dinosaur State Park, Rocky Hill, Connecticut.

A sequence of pictures showing the excavation of *Coelophysis* at Ghost Ranch, New Mexico.

Arrival at Ghost Ranch, New Mexico, for the purpose of doing some reconnaissance in the Upper Triassic Chinle Formation at the base of the cliffs, seen in the distance.

A wooden roof is built over the quarry. By now it is evident that this is a rich deposit that will require many weeks of work. Protection for the fossils being exposed, and for the diggers, is desirable.

Applying a "bandage," or "cinch," over a block containing bones. The bandage is made by dipping coarse burlap in plaster of paris. When it hardens it makes a tough casing around the specimen. The principle is the same as that for placing a cast around a broken arm or leg.

A block, encased on its top and sides with a strong bandage. Stout pieces of wood have been plastered onto the block, to give it additional strength. Before excavation the quarry had been divided into a grid system. Grid intersections are painted on the block, and these orient it with relation to contiguous blocks. Bones were so thick that the channels between blocks were cut as narrow as possible, in an effort to damage as few bones as possible. Bones encountered in the channels were removed—a tedious process. Such bones were carefully recorded, so that they could be replaced in their proper positions in the laboratory.

In the laboratory the process is reversed. The plaster cast is cut away from the block, and the long and delicate task of exposing and preserving the fossil bones begins. Preparation work in the laboratory will take many months, as compared with weeks spent in the field.

Two skeletons in one block are being cleaned. These two specimens, which are complete, are now on exhibition in New York.

LORDS OF THE JURASSIC CONTINENTS

Southern England in early Jurassic time. The large carnivorous dinosaur *Megalosaurus* is about to attack the plated ornithischian *Scelidosaurus*.

The dinosaurs that lived during late Triassic time are interesting because, among other things, they show us not only the emergence of these reptiles from thecodont ancestors, but also the general directions that dinosaurian evolution would take during the ages to follow. For the most part these early dinosaurs were not large; indeed, as we have seen, many of them were quite small and were anything but dominant in their environments. Only a few such as the prosauropods and some selected carnivores reached sizes that indicated in any way that the two following periods of geologic history together were to be an age of giants. Yet the advent of Jurassic time truly was the beginning of the age of giants, and among the giants the sauropod dinosaurs were supreme, carrying to extremes the adaptations that are exemplified in the late Triassic prosauropods. Furthermore, the sauropods *began* their long evolutionary history as giants; one might say that geologically speaking they became instantaneous giants, because the first of these great dinosaurs is found in rocks of very early Jurassic age.

The name is *Barapasaurus*, and its well-preserved remains have been found in the Lower Jurassic Kota Formation, exposed near the junction of the Godavari and Pranhita rivers, in central India. Here in a land of exotic civilizations, where domed temples rise above forests still inhabited by deer and even leopards, is a paleontological graveyard that has yielded gigantic bones, the age of which is to be measured in millions of years.

Barapasaurus is no transitional or primitive sauropod in spite of its early age; it is a fully developed member of the group, showing many of those features that are so typical of these greatest of all dinosaurs. Thus the skeleton of *Barapasaurus* is of massive proportions, fifty feet or more in length and standing some fifteen feet high at the highest point of the back, above the hips. And as is characteristic of all sauropods the limbs are massive, the feet broad and elephantine, the neck and tail very long, and the skull seemingly ridiculously small for an animal so large. In life *Barapasaurus* may have weighed as much as twenty tons—possibly more.

Barapasaurus had set a giant pattern that was to hold, with variations, from the beginning of Jurassic time until the end of Cretaceous history—a span of some one hundred twenty million years. It was a pattern of giant proportions, establishing the sauropods as remarkably massive reptiles, probably rather slow and deliberate in their movements and certainly not very intelligent. Nevertheless it was a pattern for success that may be compared after a fashion with the pattern established even earlier for the turtles. That too has been a design for massive reptiles (in their own context) living slow and seemingly uneventful lives, and persisting from the middle of the Triassic Period to the present day—a span longer than that of sauropod evolution by some eighty million years. Success is not always to the swift; there is more than a grain of truth to the old fable of the tortoise and the hare.

Large and even gigantic size became a common pattern among other dinosaurs of early Jurassic age, but of course not on such an extreme scale as characterized the sauropods. It is no surprise to find gi-

The trend to gigantic size, so characteristic of the sauropod dinosaurs, is exemplified in *Apatosaurus*, sixty feet long, fifteen feet high, and with a probable live weight of forty tons. The skeleton of a modern man illustrates dramatically the huge size of this dinosaur. *Apatosaurus* skeleton at the American Museum of Natural History, New York.

ant carnivores in Lower Jurassic rocks, because where there were large herbivores there inevitably were large predators to accompany them. A typical early Jurassic carnivore is *Megalosaurus,* as we have seen one of the first dinosaurs to be described. This widely distributed and long persisting theropod is generally somewhat larger than *Dilophosaurus* described in the previous chapter, and is qualified by the features that already have been enumerated in the account of *Dilophosaurus;* large size, an inordinately large skull, dagger-like teeth, bipedal posture, strong hind limbs with three-toed, bird-like feet, small fore limbs with three clawed fingers, and a heavy tail. *Megalosaurus* did not have the crests that decorated the skull of *Dilophosaurus,* but crests or no, it was a sufficiently fearsome predator, against whose onslaughts the herbivores of that time were constantly threatened.

Megalosaurus typifies the giant carnivorous dinosaurs; aggressive, running rapidly on its long hind limbs, and attacking its victims with powerful jaws set with dagger-like teeth.

Overleaf: Western North America in late Jurassic time when Morrison dinosaurs ruled the land. In the foreground the carnosaur *Ceratosaurus* feeds on the carcass of the sauropod *Apatosaurus,* and is joined at the feast by two little coelurosaurs, *Ornitholestes.* Dominating the scene is the huge sauropod *Brachiosaurus,* while the plated ornithischian *Stegosaurus* walks in front of it in the opposite direction. In the background, on the left, are two ornithopods, *Camptosaurus;* another *Apatosaurus* is on the far right. Primitive vegetation covers the landscape; no flowers are to be seen.

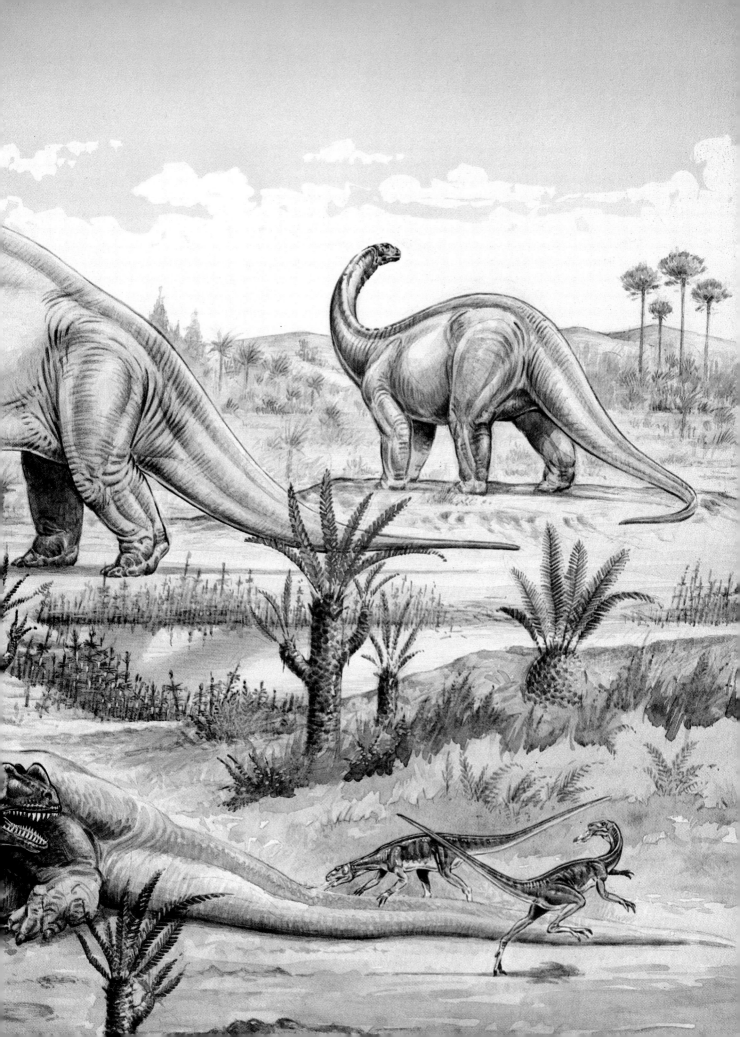

Not all of the carnivorous dinosaurs of the early Jurassic were giants; the small coelurosaurs, so widely spread across Triassic landscapes, continued into the Jurassic as is evident from some small fossils of early Jurassic age, found in western North America. There was an ecological niche for such hunters of small game, and they carried on the mode of life that had been established by their Triassic ancestors.

The picturesque little town of Lyme Regis on the Channel Coast of England is famous in the annals of paleontology. It was here in the early years of the nineteenth century that Mary Anning took over the unusual business of her dying father, which was the collecting and sale of fossils to tourists and visitors who came to southern Dorset for seaside vacations, and it was here that Mary Anning became famous among paleontologists for her discoveries of Jurassic marine reptiles.

And it was near here, close to the neighboring town of Charmouth, that the fossil remains of *Scelidosaurus* were found, thereby providing evidence for the first of the plated or armored dinosaurs. Although possibly the first ankylosaur in the strict sense of the word, there is reason to think, as has been pointed out in the previous chapter, that the ultimate origin of these reptiles may be found in the little Triassic dinosaur *Scutellosaurus*, a primitive ornithischian notable for its ample covering of armor plates. Perhaps *Scelidosaurus* and *Scutellosaurus* were descended from a common ancestor; this is a question yet to be decided. However that may be, the principle of protection by means of armor, adumbrated in the Triassic dinosaur from Arizona, was developed in *Scelidosaurus* along lines that were to prove quite successful in later Mesozoic history. As for *Scelidosaurus* such armor was obviously a distinct advantage for life in a world where megalosaurs roamed.

Scelidosaurus is about twelve feet in length, thereby showing some trend toward large or gigantic size that marked the development of dinosaurs through early Jurassic time. This dinosaur, probably because of its considerable size and its heavy coating of armor, was permanently quadrupedal, with the fore limbs shorter but not remarkably shorter than the hind limbs. The hand is thoroughly adapted for walking—a short, broad, padded hand similar to the foot. Both hand and foot were capable of supporting a heavy body; both are provided with four functional digits. The neck of *Scelidosaurus* is rather long but not excessively so, and the skull is small. In the sides of the jaws are small, spatulate teeth, not unlike those of *Scutellosaurus*, and of course the fronts of the jaws are rather beak-like. The armor of this dinosaur consists of longitudinal rows of bony scutes, those along the middle of the back and tail being pointed, to form sharp spikes.

These glimpses of early Jurassic dinosaurs—a sauropod in India, carnivores in North America and Europe, and an armored dinosaur in England—afford some clues as to the directions of dinosaurian evolution at the beginning of the age of giants. Yet they are only glimpses because the record of Lower Jurassic dinosaurs is a meagre one. It is necessary to turn to rocks of late Jurassic age for an adequate view of dinosaurian life during this period of geologic history.

The increase in dinosaurian diversity, so modestly begun with the advent of Jurassic time, continued with the progression of the period to reach a climax in the late Jurassic—the time when the Morrison Formation was deposited across large areas in western North America, when Upper Jurassic sediments were laid down by the rivers and lakes of Europe, and when the Tendaguru beds were accumulated in eastern Africa. In other areas there also were continental basins where late Jurassic dinosaurs lived, died, and were buried—for example in China, Africa, and South America. Late Jurassic time evidently was an interval of low, tropical lands across the ancient Pangaean supercontinent, a time when numerous dinosaurs moved back and forth, confined in their wandering only by the seacoasts along the edges of their homelands.

Their broad wanderings were made possible not only by the connections then existing that facilitated movements from one part of Pangaea to another, but also by the uniformity of climates that

Excavating the right hind limb of a large sauropod dinosaur near Como Bluff, Wyoming.

This parade is made up of dinosaurs that lived together, in one place and at one time. Here are some of the denizens of the Rocky Mountain states when, some one hundred fifty million years ago, this region was a low-lying, tropical land, inhabited by a varied assemblage of dinosaurs, ranging in size from huge giants—the largest animals ever to live on land—to dwarfs no larger than chickens and cranes. The fossil bones of these dinosaurs are now found in the Morrison Formation of late Jurassic age.

Dominating the scene were the saurischian giants, from left to right, *Brachiosaurus, Diplodocus,* and *Apatosaurus*. These great herbivores reached extreme weights of more than eighty tons and extreme lengths of ninety feet.

Among other herbivores were the small ornithischian *Camptosaurus,* on the left, and the bizarre, plated ornithischian *Stegosaurus*.

Bringing up the rear is *Allosaurus,* a giant saurischian carnivore that in life preyed upon other dinosaurs.

The smallest of the group is *Ornitholestes,* a saurischian carnivore that probably fed upon lizards and other small game.

We have said that some of these giant animals weighed eighty tons or more. How can we know how heavy they were?

One way is to make some educated guesses. Another is to try to determine the weights in a pragmatic fashion. An attempt to do this was made some years ago. Scale models of the various dinosaurs, carefully sculpted by first-rate artists under scientific supervision, were placed in containers and covered with fine sand. When the models were removed the volume of sand displaced by each could be measured. (Sand was used rather than water, for these displacement measurements, to obviate the possibility of water being lost because of absorption by the models.) Then, assuming the specific gravity of dinosaurs to have been slightly less than 1.00 (the specific gravity of an alligator is .89), it was possible, by scaling up the results derived from the models to life size, to arrive at reasonably realistic figures for the weights of the living dinosaurs.

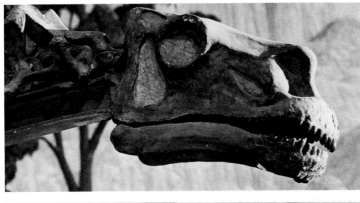

For many years the skeleton of *Apatosaurus* at Yale University was provided with an incorrectly restored skull, as seen here.

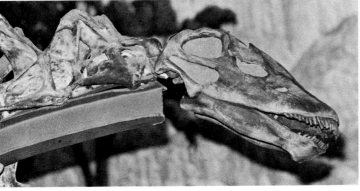

Recent studies have shown that the skull of *Apatosaurus* is more slender and with weaker teeth than was previously thought to be the case. Here is the new skull on the Yale skeleton.

prevailed throughout the world. Great expanses of land were near sea level, while tropical and subtropical climates existed from equatorial regions to high latitudes. Within this uniform world, lands were covered by primitive forests not unlike the vegetation of the later years of Triassic time. Large conifers grew across vast expanses of the earth, along with tree ferns, cycads, and other primitive plants, while the ground was covered with ferns. Even at this date, millions of years after the close of the Triassic, there were no true flowering plants and there were no grasses. In short, late Jurassic dinosaurs roamed through green forests the likes of which had been known to their distant ancestors.

A good way to become acquainted with the dinosaurs and their contemporaries of late Jurassic time is to review the fossils found in the Morrison Formation. Exposures of this geologic level are to be seen across wide areas of the western United States, and from some localities extensive collections have been made during the past century. Particularly noteworthy are the dinosaur localities in the Morrison beds of Colorado, Utah, and Wyoming, although dinosaurs and other reptiles of this age have been collected in New Mexico and some additional regions as well.

The Morrison Formation is named after the little town of Morrison, a few miles west of Denver, Colorado, where O. C. Marsh made some of his collections. Today, at the striking Red Rocks outdoor theater, north of Morrison, audiences may see, beyond the stage as they listen to symphony concerts, the ridge along which Marsh and his collectors excavated giant bones. Edward Drinker Cope, Marsh's bitter rival, and his men collected dinosaurs from near Canyon City, Colorado.

In Wyoming, the most famous locality is at Como Bluff, in the southeastern part of the state, where Marsh's men made huge collections, and where Cope parties attempted to horn in, with the resultant quarrels leading almost to open warfare. Here, too, is the famous "Quarry 9" along Como Ridge, where numerous fossils of tiny early mammals have been found.

In Utah is the famous Dinosaur National Monument, originally an extensive quarry opened and worked by Earl Douglass of the Carnegie Museum of Pittsburgh. Today this quarry is preserved within a large building, as part of the national monument,

and there visitors may see Morrison dinosaurs in place in the rocks.

Late Jurassic time was above all the age of sauropod supremacy, when giant sauropods, descended from ancestors exemplified by the early Jurassic genus *Barapasaurus*, branched out along varied lines of evolutionary development. As has been mentioned, the anatomical plan of these dinosaurs was rather consistent—gigantic body, long neck and tail, massive limbs, and a relatively small skull.

Perhaps the best known late Jurassic sauropod is *Apatosaurus*, or *Brontosaurus*, from the Morrison Formation. This dinosaur already has been described in a general way (see page 45) and little need be added at this place. One detail is, however, worthy of notice. For many years the skull of *Apatosaurus* was thought to be comparatively deep, with rather robust teeth in the front of the skull and lower jaws. This concept was based upon skulls that, it turns out, belong to another sauropod, *Camarasaurus*, found in the vicinity of *Apatosaurus* skeletons. Unfortunately no skull had been discovered in undoubted association with a skeleton. Quite recently, however, such an association has been established, from which it is seen that the skull of *Apatosaurus* is more slenderly built, with weaker teeth, than the skull formerly thought to represent this dinosaur. Indeed, the skull of *Apatosaurus* is rather similar to that of *Diplodocus*, another Morrison sauropod, to be mentioned in a following paragraph. It, like all sauropod skulls, is of archosaurian design, with openings in front of and behind the eye, and with a small braincase. Teeth are limited to the front parts of the jaws and are weak and rodlike in shape.

As for *Camarasaurus*, some skulls of which had been so mistakenly put on *Apatosaurus* skeletons in several museums, a complete skeleton with skull forms one of the choice exhibits at the Carnegie Museum. What makes this skeleton so unusual is that it belongs to a juvenile sauropod, a "teen-ager" if you will. This small camarasaur, a real rarity because juvenile sauropod skeletons are very uncommon, is only about sixteen feet in length, possibly a fourth the length of an adult, and it has the comparatively larger head and shorter neck and tail that one might expect in a young dinosaur of this type.

Diplodocus, mentioned above, and found along with other sauropod dinosaurs in the Morrison For-

It is necessary, now and then, to check a dinosaur skeleton on exhibit, to see if the bones are too dry, or cracked, or perhaps thoughtlessly damaged by inquisitive visitors.

mation, is similar in structure to *Apatosaurus*, but is remarkably slender and attenuated, so that with a length of about ninety feet it is the longest dinosaur known. Yet in life it was probably only about half the weight of sauropods such as *Apatosaurus*. The nostrils of *Diplodocus* are situated on the top of the skull, perhaps an indication that this dinosaur may have spent part of its time in lakes and rivers.

Diplodocus may have the distinction of being the world's most widely exhibited dinosaur. A beautifully complete skeleton was excavated years ago from the Carnegie Museum quarry and eventually was named *Diplodocus carnegii* by W. J. Holland of the museum. Andrew Carnegie, the patron of the museum, was extraordinarily pleased with this honor, so he instructed Dr. Holland to have casts made of the complete skeleton, to be distributed to museums around the world. It was an awesome assignment, casting numerous replicas of each of more

than two hundred bones comprising the skeleton of *Diplodocus*. But the task was in time completed under the supervision of Serafino Augustini, a master in the art of casting. Then began an international triumphal journey on the part of Dr. Holland, escorting casts of the skeletons to museums in many lands, where at each institution there were ceremonies at which Holland often received medals and honorary degrees. The first cast was presented to the British Museum (Natural History) in London, where today it forms a centerpiece in the great entrance hall. Museums in Berlin, Frankfurt-on-Main, Vienna, Bologna, Paris, La Plata, and Mexico City also received casts. Finally, long after the expansive years of Andrew Carnegie, the molds for the skeleton were sent to Utah, where today a cast, made in cement, can be seen standing outside the Utah Field House in Vernal.

Brachiosaurus, a giant among giants, has been

Diplodocus is the longest but not the most massive of the sauropod dinosaurs. This skeleton, about ninety feet long, was collected at Dinosaur National Monument, Utah, and is on display at the Smithsonian Institution, Washington, D.C.

A heavy dinosaur bone in a plaster jacket
is carried back to camp at Tendaguru.

A large dinosaur leg bone as it was first
seen at Tendaguru, Tanzania. The dig was
of gigantic proportions and yielded gigantic
bones.

Dr. James A. Jensen of Brigham Young University collects giant dinosaurs from the Morrison Formation in Colorado.

The excavation of a dinosaur is a major undertaking involving special skills and equipment. First the "overburden"— rock above the bone layer—must be removed, with a bulldozer if possible. Hard rock immediately above the bones is now being broken up with a gasoline-powered jackhammer. Note the string of sauropod tail vertebrae in the foreground.

A pneumatic chisel is here being used to break up the rock surrounding the bones, thereby exposing them. In the background are bones already exposed.

When the bones are first exposed they are frequently cracked and shattered. Any attempt to remove this bone without using tested paleontological techniques would be disastrous.

Shellac is poured on the exposed bone to harden it.

After the shellac has dried, the bone is encased in a heavy bandage of burlap and plaster of paris. (Often a separator such as tissue or Japanese rice paper is applied over the bone.)

Large bones are strengthened by "splints"—heavy lengths of wood—bound into the plastered fossil. Here a nine-foot-long shoulder blade is being encased. It will be taken to the laboratory where the bandages will be removed and the bone carefully cleaned and preserved.

The skeletons seen on page 91 brought to life by the renowned artist Charles R. Knight. *Allosaurus* is stripping meat from the carcass of *Apatosaurus*.

found not only in the Morrison beds but also in the Tendaguru beds of what is now Tanzania, in eastern Africa. In fact, the finest skeleton of this dinosaur, collected in Africa before the First World War, is now on display at the museum in East Berlin. The skull of this dinosaur towers forty feet above the floor of the exhibition hall, partly because this is a big dinosaur and is mounted with the head raised, and partly because in *Brachiosaurus*, as distinct from most of the other sauropods, the fore limbs are much longer than the hind limbs, so that the back slopes, giraffe-fashion, to the rear. In this dinosaur

the nasal openings are very large and placed high on the skull; it is thought that perhaps one function of such nostrils was in cooling the brain. It has been estimated that *Brachiosaurus* had a live weight of some eighty tons, which was assumed—for a time—to be the top limit of weight for a land-living animal.

Yet within recent years the bones of a brachiosaur-type sauropod even larger than *Brachiosaurus* have been excavated by James Jensen of Brigham Young University from the Morrison beds of western Colorado. This brachiosaur, as yet not named but going by the nickname of "Ultrasaurus," has a shoulder blade eight feet in length, while a single vertebra from the neck is five feet long. If *Brachiosaurus* weighed eighty tons, then this even larger sauropod may have weighed one hundred tons. It surely would seem to represent the ultimate in size for a land-living animal.

Although the sauropods were preeminent in Morrison times, they shared their environment with other large and small dinosaurs. Where there are giant herbivores there are giant carnivores to prey upon them, and this was especially true in the Jurassic world. *Allosaurus*, a Morrison dinosaur, is in effect an enlarged version of its European predecessor and contemporary *Megalosaurus*. This giant carnosaur was perhaps an active predator and at the same time a carrion-eater. (We know that numerous modern predators, even the majestic lion, do not disdain carrion when such is easily available. One rule for many a successful carnivore is to make use of opportunities as they arise.) The skull of *Allosaurus* is very large, thereby giving a wide gape to the jaws, which would be advantageous for feeding upon large game. The teeth are dagger-like. The long, strong hind limbs carried *Allosaurus* across the land at considerable speed; the hind feet have three toes each and are bird-like. The fore limbs are small, yet strong, and the three fingers of each hand are armed with long, curved claws, which must have been used as aids in the capture of prey. The heavy tail served to counterbalance the body, pivoted as it was at the hips. That *Allosaurus* fed upon such large dinosaurs as *Apatosaurus* is suggested by a partial skeleton of this sauropod at the American Museum of Natural History in New York, in which the spines of a number of vertebrae were bitten off, the tooth marks on these damaged vertebrae exactly matching the spacing of the teeth in an *Allosaurus* skull.

A supposedly distinct Morrison carnivore, perhaps in life a rival of *Allosaurus*, is *Ceratosaurus*, much like *Allosaurus* as to size and general build, but distinguished, among other things, by the presence of a horn on the nose. It has been suggested, however, that this carnivore may in fact be *Allosaurus* with an abnormal growth that looks like a horn,

The giant carnivore *Allosaurus* is here posed as if feeding on the backbone of *Apatosaurus*, the vertebral spines of which have been bitten off. The tooth marks on the vertebrae match the spacing of the teeth in *Allosaurus*. Exhibit at the American Museum of Natural History, New York.

or that possibly it may be a male *Allosaurus.* Let us at the moment consider the true nature of *Ceratosaurus* as an open question.

Not all of the late Jurassic carnivores were giants. *Ornitholestes,* another Morrison dinosaur, is a small coelurosaur, its skeleton being no more than about six feet in length. In general it has the proportions and adaptations that we have seen so characteristic of Triassic coelurosaurs such as *Coelophysis,* so its features need not be recounted at length here. However, the fore limb is somewhat larger, relatively speaking, than is the case in *Coelophysis,* and the three elongated fingers are so arranged that the first finger, or "thumb," is somewhat opposed to the other two. This suggests that *Ornitholestes* (the name means "bird-robber") preyed upon small animals, perhaps lizards rather than birds, often catching them and holding them in its hands.

That small coelurosaurians did eat lizards is defi-nitely proven by the beautiful skeleton of *Compsognathus,* found in the fine-grained Upper Jurassic lithographic limestone of Bavaria. This, one of the smallest of all known dinosaurs, is no larger than a domestic chicken. (In form it is again in general a replica of earlier coelurosaurs, an example of the fact that primitive animals can persist for long ages, living with their descendents, so to speak, and be quite successful. Look at the American opossum, essentially a Cretaceous mammal that does very well in the modern world.) The relevant thing about the skeleton of *Compsognathus* is that within its body cavity is the skeleton of a small Jurassic lizard, quite obviously an undigested meal.

So far our attention has been devoted to the saurischian dinosaurs of late Jurassic time; these dinosaurs, particularly the sauropods, were predominant in the reptilian assemblages represented by fossils from the Morrison beds, as well as from oth-

Ceratosaurus, a giant carnivorous dinosaur with a horn on its nose. Exhibit at the Smithsonian Institution, Washington, D.C.

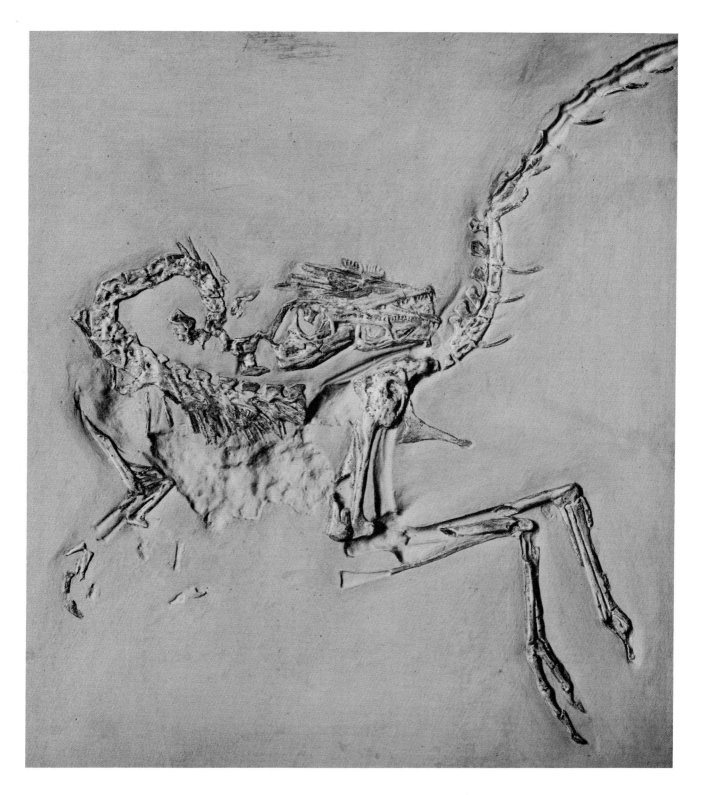

Compsognathus, a dinosaur about the size of a chicken, as preserved in the lithographic limestone of Solnhofen, Bavaria, Germany.

93

Two skeletons of the generalized ornithischian dinosaur *Camptosaurus*. The differences in size probably represent differences in individual ages. Exhibit at the Smithsonian Institution, Washington, D.C.

er Jurassic localities. There were, however, some important ornithischian dinosaurs in the late Jurassic scene.

A characteristic ornithischian dinosaur in the Morrison deposits, and in other Upper Jurassic beds as well, is *Camptosaurus*, a rather generalized ornithopod. *Camptosaurus* is a small to medium-sized ornithischian, the larger individuals reaching lengths of twelve to fifteen feet. It shows no remarkable specializations; it was in life dominantly bipedal, but not exclusively so, because the fore limbs are sufficiently large so that this dinosaur could walk very comfortably in a quadrupedal position. The body and tail, limbs and feet of *Camptosaurus* are rather heavy; they do not show the slender grace of the theropod limbs, so it would seem likely that this dinosaur was not so agile as the carnivores, especially the small carnivores that lived in late Jurassic time. The skull of *Camptosaurus*, al-

though of basic archosaurian structure, does not have the large opening in front of the eye that is so prominent in the theropod dinosaurs. Here we see a trend that was to mark the course of ornithischian evolution—the reduction and sometimes the elimination of openings in the skull, other than those for the eyes and nostrils.

If *Camptosaurus* is to be described as generalized, the same is not to be said of *Stegosaurus*, a remarkably bizarre ornithischian from the Morrison beds. This is a large dinosaur, twenty feet or more in length, with long hind limbs, and short fore limbs only half the length of the limbs in back. Yet this dinosaur was completely quadrupedal; consequently the back is strongly arched, rising from the low shoulder region to the high hips and then dropping again to the tip of the tail. The limbs are heavy, the feet are short and broad, and the five fingers of the fore foot and the three functional toes of the hind foot terminate in sharp hooves. The skull of *Stegosaurus* is small, essentially a somewhat elongated camptosaur skull. And as in *Camptosaurus* the fronts of the jaws lack teeth and are in the form of a beak.

The most striking features of *Stegosaurus* are the large, triangular upright plates forming a double row along the back and the tail, and the four sharp spikes at the end of the tail. The plates of *Stegosaurus* are thick at the base and thin along the edges, and are traversed by branching furrows running from the bases to the edges. It would seem evident that the thick bases of the plates were imbedded in the skin of the back, and that the furrows in the bone contained blood vessels. When the first skeletons of *Stegosaurus* were discovered it was thought that the plates were arranged in pairs along the back. Then a skeleton was found with the plates more or less in position above the vertebrae, but arranged alternately, so there was a tendency on the part of many paleontologists to regard this alternate arrangement as correct. But can this be the case? Bilateral symmetry is a rule among animals with backbones, and it does seem strange that such bilateral symmetry should be violated in the case of

Stegosaurus as displayed at the Smithsonian Institution, Washington, D.C. Note the large plates on the back placed in alternating positions. Perhaps such an arrangement (if valid) allowed for efficient absorption and dissipation of heat.

A late Jurassic confrontation in western North America between the carnivore *Allosaurus* and the plated ornithischian *Stegosaurus*.

CRETACEOUS CULMINATION OF THE DINOSAURS

The ornithopod dinosaur *Iguanodon,* of early Cretaceous age, stood some fifteen feet high and was over thirty feet in length. This bipedal reptile walked on powerful hind limbs to browse on the leaves of early deciduous trees and bushes, the numerous teeth being well adapted to such a diet. Large spikes were borne on the thumbs and evidently were used for defense.

The stegosaurs held on into Cretaceous time, but their history in this last of the Mesozoic periods was short and relatively unimportant. Perhaps their strong specializations, so apparent in what seems to us the bizarre appearance of *Stegosaurus,* were not particularly suited to the new and very different environments that so clearly distinguished Cretaceous landscapes from those of the preceeding Jurassic Period. For the opening of the Cretaceous Period was marked by a profound revolution in plant life resulting in the establishment of flowering angiosperms across the continents.

Overleaf: Southeastern England in early Cretaceous time. Two small ornithopods, *Hypsilophodon,* browse in the right foreground, while the armored ornithischian *Polacanthus* walks behind them. On the left are two large ornithopods of the genus *Iguanodon,* the first dinosaur to be described. A carnivore, *Altispinax,* is seen in the distance.

So it was that the forests within which *Allosaurus* and *Apatosaurus* and *Stegosaurus* sought their living gave way to new forests, woodlands of colorful, progressive plants, replacing the monotonously green and primitive jungles of former ages. The dinosaurs that succeeded the lords of the Jurassic world wandered among flowering magnolias and willow trees, sassafras, poplars, oaks, vibernum, clinging grape vines, fig trees, and a host of other deciduous plants, intermixed in many areas with pines and cycads persisting from former times. Here was an abundant new supply of food for plant-eating animals; consequently new ornithischian herbivores appeared to share this plant world with some persisting sauropods, left over from the days of their Jurassic dominance.

A sampling of Lower Cretaceous dinosaurs from various parts of the world will give some idea as to the directions of dinosaurian evolution at this stage of geologic history, directions that were determined to a large degree by the revolution in plant life that so distinguished Cretaceous environments, even those of early Cretaceous age, from the more primitive environments of the Jurassic and before that the Triassic Periods. To begin this sampling, we may look at *Iguanodon*, Gideon Mantell's dinosaur from the Lower Cretaceous rocks of southern England.

Iguanodon, as indicated on page 48, is closely related to *Camptosaurus;* in fact one might consider *Iguanodon* as a camptosaur grown to giant proportions, and specialized in certain respects. In spite of its large size, *Iguanodon* was dominantly a bipedal dinosaur, but like *Camptosaurus*, it probably would come down on all four feet on numerous occasions. The hind limbs are strong and massive, well adapted for the support of a bulky animal, and terminate in heavy, three-toed feet with robust claws. The tail is very heavy, to serve not only as a counterbalance to the body, but also as a prop when *Iguanodon* was standing high on its hind limbs to browse on the succulent leaves of deciduous trees. An interesting feature of this dinosaur is the presence of numerous ossified tendons running along the back and the tail in a sort of lattice-work pattern, quite obviously to strengthen the backbone. The fore limbs are very strong and the broad fore feet have five functional digits. A striking character of *Iguanodon* is the spike-like thumb, which Richard Owen

had supposed was a nasal horn; of course this idea was laid to rest when the articulated skeletons of *Iguanodon* were brought up out of the Belgian mine. This formidable spike must have been a defensive weapon; *Iguanodon* otherwise was a peaceful herbivore, relying in the main on its large size for protection. For although it was bipedal it probably was a clumsy and rather slow biped, possibly not able to run rapidly enough to escape the onslaughts of the active and aggressive carnosaurs that lived in its world.

The front of the skull and jaws of *Iguanodon* are in the form of a strong beak, while along the sides of the upper and lower jaws are rows of specialized teeth, each tooth carrying some heavy, vertical ridges on its outer surface, while the edges of the tooth are crenulated with numerous little cusplets. These teeth may have been derived from the simpler cusped teeth that we have seen in some of the primitive ornithischian dinosaurs, such as *Scutellosaurus* or *Lesothosaurus*. When worn by abrasion, the teeth of *Iguanodon* formed extensive surfaces for the chopping and grinding of plant food.

In the same sediments that contain *Iguanodon*, there has been found the primitive ornithopod dinosaur known as *Hypsilophodon*, which until the discovery of the Upper Triassic ornithischian dinosaurs earlier described was generally regarded as the most primitive of known ornithopods—a nice example of the fact that primitive animals often survive very successfully, to live as it were alongside their specialized descendants. *Hypsilophodon* is a small, lightly built ornithopod, about five feet in length. The skull is rather similar to that in the Triassic ornithischians, particularly *Lesothosaurus*, and the teeth in the sides of the jaws are of primitive ornithischian form. However, there are some small teeth in the front of the upper jaws, an atavistic character. An interesting feature of *Hypsilophodon* is the presence of two rows of small armor plates along the back, which would seem to be the remnants of an early condition such as we saw in *Scutellosaurus*, or beyond that, in the armored thecodont reptiles.

The hind limbs of *Hypsilophodon* are long and slender, the fore limbs are relatively small, indications that this dinosaur was a confirmed biped, always walking on the hind limbs. It was long advocated by some paleontologists that this little dinosaur was able to climb trees, largely on the evi-

jaws in the hadrosaurian dinosaurs are devoid of teeth, the sides of the upper and lower jaws are liberally supplied with teeth of complex form and arrangement. These "dental batteries" (as they are called) of the hadrosaurs are mechanisms for the chopping and grinding of plant food that have seldom been equaled in the animal world.

Each dental battery, above and below in the sides of the jaws, is so complex that one must see it, or a picture of it, to properly understand its form and function. A brief description will be attempted at this place.

The individual teeth of the dentition are, when viewed from the side, shaped like vertically elongated diamonds or lozenges, with rounded ends and sides, and with a long, low ridge running down the middle of each tooth. From this lozenge the tooth extends down (or up) in a long, tapering root. In each battery there is a succession of such teeth overlapping each other and forming a vertical row, and in each battery the teeth of the vertical rows alternate in arrangement from front to back. Each vertical row contains from four to six teeth. There are as many as forty or even sixty rows of teeth forming each battery.

During life there was a constant eruption of teeth, the teeth of the upper battery pushing down, those of the lower battery pushing up. As the teeth erupted above the margins of the jaws those in the upper and lower batteries ground against each other to form a long grinding surface—a sort of mill. And the difference in hardness of the enamel forming the tooth's lateral surface and the dentine of the rest of the tooth contributed to the efficiency of the

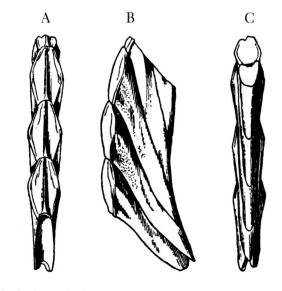

A single vertical tooth row of the Upper Cretaceous hadrosaur *Kritosaurus,* as seen in (A) lingual or inner view, (B) posterior or back view, and (C) buccal or outer view.

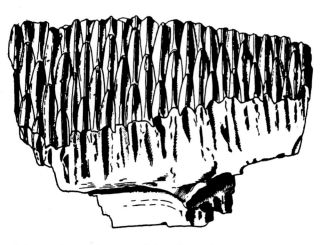

A lower dental battery of the Upper Cretaceous hadrosaur *Kritosaurus,* showing the alternating succession of the vertical tooth rows.

The lower jaw of the hadrosaur *Anatosaurus* as seen in lingual view. This shows the position of the large, complex tooth battery within the jaw.

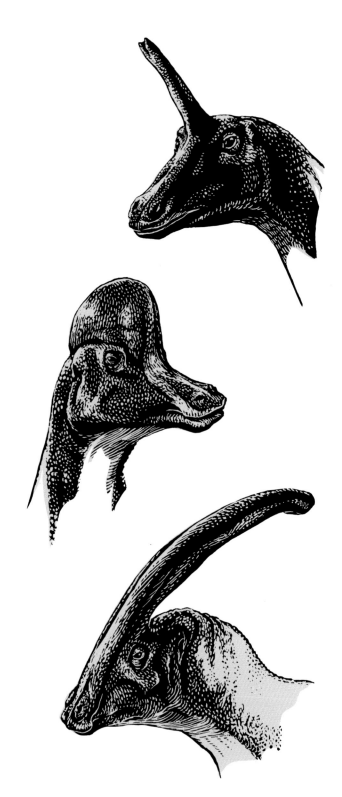

mill. As each tooth was worn down its remnants finally dropped out of the jaw, but it was at the same time being replaced by the tooth above or below it. And since the tooth rows are arranged alternately, there were never any gaps caused by replacement. There was a constant flow of replacing teeth to occupy the positions of those teeth lost by wear.

Since there are forty and up to sixty rows of teeth, with as many as six successional teeth in each vertical row, there may be from one hundred fifty to three hundred fifty teeth in each dental battery of an advanced hadrosaur. Four such batteries, one on each side, above and below, thus make a total of from six hundred to twelve hundred or more teeth, an impressive number indeed for the handling of harsh plant food.

Is this description understandable? Look at the illustrations; they should help to make clear the arrangement of teeth in a hadrosaur skull and jaw.

We now come to those aspects of the skull that lend such great variety to the hadrosaurian dinosaurs—the differences caused by some remarkable developments of the premaxillary and nasal bones that surround the nasal openings. Three groups of hadrosaurs may be discerned, according to the manner in which these bones are arranged and developed.

The first group is that of the flat-headed hadrosaurs, in which the premaxillary and nasal bones are located at the front of the skull, surrounding the nasal openings, as would be expected in a normal backboned animal.

The second group is comprised of the solid-crested hadrosaurs, in which the two bones are modified in such a way that although still surrounding the nasal openings they are enlarged over the top of the skull to form a crest. In some of these solid-crested hadrosaurs the crest is small, in others it is in-

Crest patterns in late Cretaceous hadrosaurs.
    At the top is *Tsintaosaurus* from China, with a solid upright spike on the head, perhaps for display. (This spike seems too fragile to have served as a defensive horn.) In the middle is *Corythosaurus* from Alberta, with a large hollow crest that in life housed a loop of the nasal passage. At the bottom is *Parasaurolophus* from New Mexico, with an elongated hollow crest, also containing in life a long loop of the nasal passage. Perhaps these hollow crests allowed for a sophisticated sense of smell or for a resonant voice, or both.

creased in size, especially by a backward prolongation of the nasal bone, to form a pointed, horn-like spike, extending above the skull. In one hadrosaur from China, *Tsintaosaurus*, this nasal spike is very long, rising vertically from the skull roof above the eyes, and is divided, or bifurcated, at its end, like a two-tined fork.

The third group is made up of the hollow-crested hadrosaurs, in which the premaxillary and nasal bones are enlarged and expanded in such a way as to form a large, hollow crest on the top of the skull, housing a loop of the nasal passage. In these dinosaurs the elongated nasal passage entered the crest, to loop through it and then descend into the throat to meet the upper end of the trachea, or windpipe.

What is the meaning of the crests in the solid-crested and hollow-crested hadrosaurs? As for the first group, one may only suppose that the crest was some sort of a display structure. It is too small in some of these hadrosaurs, and where enlarged, seemingly too weak, to have functioned as any kind of a "horn" useful in combat. This is especially true for *Tsintaosaurus*, mentioned above, in which the crest forms a slender projection above the skull— decorative but not robust.

As for the hollow-crested hadrosaurs, the crests may have served in part for display, but they seem too complex merely for display. The expansion of the nasal passage into the crest must have had some significance. It has been suggested that this expanded nasal loop was an accessory air storage chamber, to augment the lungs when the animal was submerged. But such an explanation involves a difficult mechanical problem—that of pulling air from the crest into the lungs. Moreover, the volume of air that might have been so stored would have been quite small as compared with lung capacity. Perhaps the best suggestions are that the expansion of the nasal passage in the crest may have served either or both of two purposes. In the first place, it may have allowed for a large mucous surface, thereby enhancing the sense of smell. Secondly, it may have provided a resonating chamber for vocalization, somewhat parallel in some respects to the great throat pouches of the modern-day howler monkey of Central America.

Our knowledge of dinosaurs is based primarily upon the fossil skeletons of these great reptiles, to a lesser degree upon the tracks they made, the nests some of them built, and even the eggs that are sometimes found within such nests. Our knowledge of the hadrosaurs, however, goes beyond the fossil remains and indications mentioned above, because certain of these dinosaurs are known from fossilized mummies showing the pattern and texture of the skin. Perhaps the finest such mummy is that of *Anatosaurus*, to be seen at the American Museum of Natural History in New York.

A natural "mummy" of the Upper Cretaceous hadrosaur *Anatosaurus,* as displayed at the American Museum of Natural History in New York. After death the carcass of this dinosaur evidently dried up so that the skin became hard. The body was then buried and the bones together with large areas of skin were fossilized.

This mummy preserves the remains of a dinosaur, the carcass of which was dessicated in dry air after the death of the animal—a case similar to what is seen today on the high plains, for example, where the dried-up skin of a rabbit or a coyote may be found, hard as a drumhead and often with some of the bones contained inside. Fortunately the hadrosaur carcass was not torn to pieces by scavengers, but was buried by rapidly accumulating sands to be fossilized, so that not only the bones of this specimen were transformed into rock but also the same happened to the skin. All of the details are there.

The skin is leathery and consists of a ground area of small tubercles, something like what is seen in a modern lizard such as a Gila monster. Within this area of tuberculated skin are clusters of flat tubercles, or little plates, if so they may be called, arranged rather regularly over the surface of the body. Between the toes of the front feet are webs of skin, giving the hand a mitten-like appearance, while down the middle of the back, from the head to the tail, is a fold of skin.

From such a mummy we can make a detailed reconstruction of what the dinosaur looked like in life, with a high degree of confidence. All that is lacking is the color, and here one may speculate that the clusters of tubercles indicate a color pattern. But that is only conjecture.

Other duck-billed dinosaur specimens show large areas of fossilized skin—notably a *Corythosaurus* from the Oldman Formation, also at the American Museum in New York. Because of the nature of the sediments in which it was found it seems possible that this mummy was preserved under somewhat wetter conditions than those prevailing when the *Anatosaurus* mummy was buried.

Having made this side excursion, so to speak, to look at the hadrosaurs in general terms, we may now return to the Oldman Formation, from which an impressive array of these dinosaurs is known. All three groups of hadrosaurs lived during Oldman time, the flat-headed ones, as represented by *Kritosaurus*, the solid-crested hadrosaurs as seen in *Prosaurolophus*, and the hollow-crested forms, represented by *Corythosaurus, Lambeosaurus*, and

Part of the fossilized skin of the *Anatosaurus* mummy seen in the preceding illustration. This shows the "pebbly" surface of the leathery skin. The clusters, or rosettes, of larger skin bumps may be indicative of a color pattern.

some horns. The horns and the frills probably were more commonly used in territorial and sexual combat.

Once more a side excursion will be made—this time for a somewhat extended look at the horned dinosaurs and their evolutionary history. It is a complex story that deserves more than passing attention. Let us begin at the beginning.

On page 52 the little Mongolian dinosaur *Psittacosaurus* was cited as representing the eleventh group of dinosaurian categories there being described. This small, early Cretaceous dinosaur, in many respects showing the features of a primitive ornithopod, is noteworthy because the front of the skull is deep and narrow, like the beak of a parrot, while the back of the skull is broad. These are the very characters that might be expected in a ceratopsian ancestor, and while *Psittacosaurus* may not be on the direct line to the horned dinosaurs, it probably is not far removed from that line.

Another Mongolian ornithischian, *Protoceratops*, which possibly might have been derived from a *Psittacosaurus*-like ancestor, in turn nicely fills the role of a ceratopsian ancestor. *Protoceratops* is a small dinosaur, the skeleton of which is about six feet in length. At least a third of this length is occupied by the skull which has a well-developed frill formed by the parietal and squamosal bones—bones that in more "normal" skulls form the roof of the braincase and a part of the side of the skull, respectively. In *Protoceratops* the frill is pierced by two large openings, or fenestrae ("windows"), one on each side within its back part. Openings such as these are passed on to the later and more advanced horned dinosaurs except for one, *Triceratops*, in which the frill is solid. The front of the skull of *Protoceratops* is narrow, to form a characteristic ceratopsian type of beak, and on top of this beak there is a little knob, the beginning of the ceratopsian horn. In the sides of the skull and jaws are lanceolate teeth, somewhat like the teeth seen in primitive ornithischian dinosaurs, evidently for the cut-

Two skeletons of the ancestral ceratopsian, or horned dinosaur, *Protoceratops,* from the Cretaceous beds of Mongolia. In this earliest ceratopsian, about six feet in length, the frill at the back of the skull already is enlarged, but no real horns are apparent. A reconstructed nest of eggs is shown.

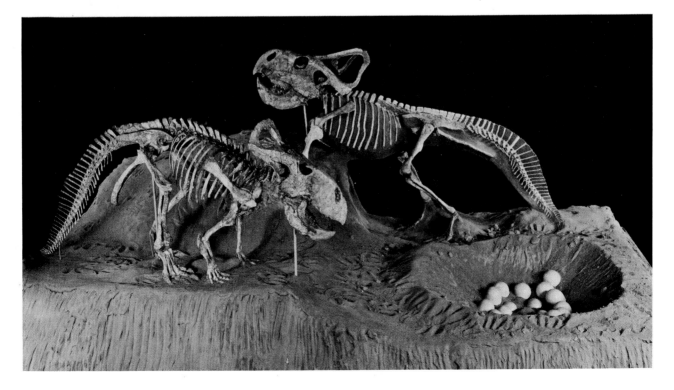

124

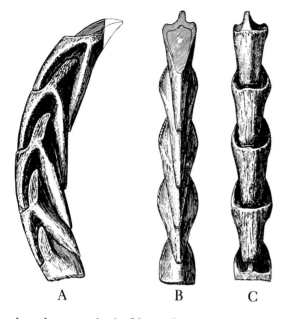

Tooth replacement in the Upper Cretaceous horned dinosaur *Triceratops*. This shows a single vertical tooth row in (A) posterior or back view, (B) buccal or external view, and (C) lingual or inner view. Note how in **A** the tip of each replacing tooth is embraced by the roots of the preceding tooth.

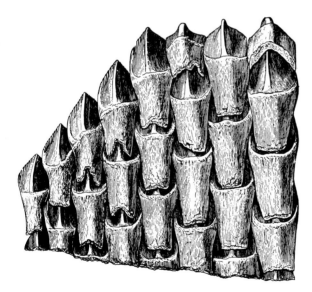

Part of a dental battery of *Triceratops* in lingual or inner view, showing the alternating succession of teeth.

ting up of plant food. These comparatively primitive teeth adumbrate the dental batteries of later ceratopsians.

A skull of such size as that seen in *Protoceratops* would have precluded any attempts at bipedal locomotion; it would have been too heavy and ungainly to be supported at the end of a raised backbone. So it is not surprising that the limbs in *Protoceratops* are fully adapted to a quadrupedal gait, the toes of both fore and hind feet being provided with little hooves. The tail is rather long.

Protoceratops was discovered in Mongolia by the Central Asiatic expeditions of the American Museum of Natural History at a locality in the Gobi known as Djadochta, where sheer cliffs of red sandstone rise from the desert to form a spectacular landmark, a flaming-red castellated butte as seen in the light of the setting sun. Here was found a prodigious wealth of *Protoceratops*, skulls and skeletons of animals of all ages, from newly hatched individuals to fully adult males and females. And what especially was exciting was the discovery at this place of nests containing the eggs of *Protoceratops*. These nests are circular, and in them there had been deposited concentric rows of elliptical eggs, having roughly striated shells, in some of which are fragmentary embryo bones. Evidently the female *Protoceratops* had come here to reproduce, scooping out hollows in the sand to receive the eggs, and covering each nest with sand, to be incubated by the heat of the sun, just as crocodiles and turtles do today. But some eggs never hatched and were fossilized, which was fortunate for people interested in dinosaurs. These were the first fossil eggs definitely to be associated with dinosaurs.

There is a considerable array of small ceratopsians from Mongolia that are related to *Protoceratops*, some even smaller than and more primitive than *Protoceratops*. Also there is a small ceratopsian from the Edmonton Formation of Alberta, which lies above the Oldman beds and consequently is younger. This little ceratopsian, *Leptoceratops*, is more primitive than *Protoceratops* in that it has a less developed frill. Once again we see a nice example of a primitive animal persisting through time to live alongside its descendants, the large horned dinosaurs such as those found in the Oldman and younger formations.

Most of these later ceratopsians will not be discussed at this place; to do so might entangle the reader in a morass of confusing details. Suffice it to say that they were numerous and varied, some with long frills, others with short frills, some with large nasal horns and small brow horns, others with large brow horns and short nasal horns. They present us with a variety of forms, especially as regards the development of the horns, that may be compared with antelopes of the modern African plains, with their differently shaped horns. Perhaps one sees similar evolutionary pressures being exerted in both instances—separated though they may be by millions of years of time. (One ceratopsian from the Edmonton Formation, *Pachyrhinosaurus*, lacks horns, but instead has a massive, raised boss on the top of the skull, above the eyes. Perhaps this ceratopsian was a butting reptile, as were the pachycephalosaurs, yet of a different type.)

Of all the horned dinosaurs, perhaps *Triceratops* is the best known to the general public. This large, solid-frilled ceratopsian, with long brow horns and a short nasal horn, epitomizes to many people the entire series of horned dinosaurs. Therefore something might be said at this place about the teeth in *Triceratops*, since they are typical of the teeth in all of the large ceratopsians. We saw that the teeth in the duck-billed dinosaurs are contained within complex batteries, in which there was a constant succession of teeth arranged in alternate rows. Much the same arrangement is seen in *Triceratops* and other large ceratopsians, except that the teeth are perhaps not so numerous as are those of the hadrosaurs. But the individual ceratopsian teeth are more complex than are hadrosaurian teeth, because each tooth is divided at its upper end (in the upper jaw) and its lower end (in the lower jaw) into two

The skeleton of the Upper Cretaceous horned dinosaur *Triceratops,* as displayed at the Smithsonian Institution in Washington, D.C.

The late Cretaceous dinosaurs of North America had evolved along varied lines of adaptation for different modes of life. This scene, in what is now Wyoming, shows two saurischian carnivores; the lightly built *Struthiomimus* in the left foreground, the giant predator *Tyrannosaurus* on the right. The other dinosaurs are all ornithischian herbivores; the armored *Ankylosaurus* in the right foreground, and from left to right in the background the dome-headed *Pachycephalosaurus*, the hadrosaur *Anatosaurus*, and the horned ceratopsian *Triceratops*.

roots; one exterior, one interior. In the vertical row of replacing teeth the crown of each successive tooth is positioned between the roots of the tooth it is to replace. Again, perhaps an illustration will make the matter more understandable than can be accomplished with mere words.

Triceratops is not only the best known of the horned dinosaurs but also perhaps the most abundant so far as fossils are concerned. Remains of *Tri-* *ceratops* are found in profusion in the uppermost Cretaceous Lance Formation, a seeming indication that this dinosaur lived in great numbers. Perhaps it roamed the hills and valleys of western North America in great herds during those final years of Cretaceous history. It would seem to have been successful in every sense of the word, and then almost like the bison of western North America, it disappeared dramatically and with extreme suddenness. We know what brought about the near extinction of the bison; we can only guess at the causes for the absolute disappearance of the last of the horned dinosaurs, *Triceratops*.

Nothing has as yet been said about the giant sauropod dinosaurs of late Cretaceous time. It would appear that these dinosaurs were greatly diminished in North America, being presently known only from scattered remains. They were, however, well represented in other regions of the world, notably in Argentina, parts of Asia, Egypt, southern Africa, Madagascar, and Europe. It should be said that in southern France are found bones of a sauropod, *Hypselosaurus*, while within the same sediments are numerous eggs—about the size of large grapefruit—that may be attributed to this dinosaur. Generally speaking, the sauropods of late Cretaceous age carried into this final stage of the Age of

The Upper Cretaceous carnosaur *Tyrannosaurus* from the Hell Creek Formation of Montana, as displayed at the American Museum of Natural History in New York. This largest of all carnivorous dinosaurs stands about eighteen feet tall and is forty feet or more in length.

The dinosaurs of the late Cretaceous Oldman fauna lived in woodlands that would seem familiar to our eyes. Along the low banks of the braided rivers were dense growths of cattails and scouring rushes, while in the streams there were colorful water lilies, adding a touch of tranquility to a scene that was not always tranquil. Sycamore saplings grew with their roots close to the water; back from the riverbanks were extensive groves of breadfruit trees, large sycamores, and tall torreyas bearing plum-like fruits, as well as numerous evergreens. Many of the trees were festooned with grapevines, and figs grew abundantly. Around the edges of the groves were thickets of katsura trees, along with china firs. In the shade of the forest the ground was covered with ferns and arum plants, including calla lilies. These were luxuriant forests, providing the food that maintained a large population of herbivorous dinosaurs.

The evidence would seem to indicate that these dinosaurs were remarkably abundant, much more so than the plant-eating animals that one may see today in an African game park. Perhaps this abundance of foraging dinosaurs may be attributed to their probable ectothermy; for if they required in general only a fraction of the food as would endothermic animals of similar size, they could have lived as dense and crowded populations in an environment where food was plentiful. It seems likely that they got much of their sustenance from the woody plants that surrounded them. Where there was such an abundance of plant-eating dinosaurs there was a plentiful array of big carnivores to prey upon the browsers. This earth was the domain of giants, in astounding numbers.

Yet impressive as they were, the dinosaurs were not the only inhabitants of the Oldman landscape. There were turtles, crocodiles, and other reptiles (pictured, a champsosaur swims away from a carnivorous dinosaur, *Albertosaurus*), while in the undergrowth, not immediately visible, were great hosts of tiny, primitive mammals. Flying reptiles soared through the air, sharing this element with toothed birds.

Angiosperms, the flowering plants, burst upon the world scene in early Cretaceous time, when dinosaurs roamed the continents in great numbers but in limited variety. The revolution in plant life consequent upon the rise of the angiosperms was quickly followed (in a geological sense) by a renaissance among the dinosaurs. Here was a new, varied, and abundant food supply for herbivores, and there was a burgeoning of plant-eating dinosaurs in response to expanded opportunities for dinosaurian life as it had never been lived before; the variety and numbers of the herbivores grew beyond anything previously existing.

Cretaceous time was in a sense the golden age of the dinosaurs; these great reptiles, living in forests of modern aspect, would seem to have been assured of life everlasting. But soon they were to disappear from the earth.

Dinosaurs the same adaptations that had made them so successful in earlier times, especially in late Jurassic history. But again, as in early Cretaceous time, they did not dominate the faunas as they had during late Jurassic years. They were in a sense overwhelmed, perhaps crowded out of feeding grounds, by the smaller but highly diverse ornithischian herbivores.

Up to this point our discussion of late Cretaceous dinosaurs has been devoted to the plant eaters, so numerous and varied at this stage of earth history. We have been somewhat in the position of a modern visitor to one of the great African game parks, where the eye is attracted to the constantly changing multitudes of herbivores, feeding in harmonious proximity, with seldom a glimpse of the carnivores that get their support from these herds. Yet the visitor knows the carnivores are there, biding their time.

The late Cretaceous carnivores certainly were there, and again a comparison may be made with modern Africa. The larger carnivores of the bushveldt are restricted in variety and few in numbers as compared with the antelopes and other herbivores on which they feed. Lions, leopards, cheetahs, hyaenas, hunting dogs, and jackals constitute most of the roll call, to be contrasted with the scores of grazing and browsing species that cover the Afri-

can plains and savannas. So it was in Oldman time. Two or three kinds of large carnosaurs preyed upon a variety of herbivorous dinosaurs, and some smaller flesh-eaters probably lived off of lizards and other small game that dwelt in the underbrush.

The dominant carnivore in the Oldman scene is *Albertosaurus*, a giant predator well adapted to hunt down large prey. (This dinosaur has in the past been designated by the names of *Gorgosaurus*, *Aublysodon*, and *Deinodon*, but now some knowledgeable paleontologists contend that it should be known as *Albertosaurus*. Although *Gorgosaurus* is well entrenched in the literature, the more correct name will here be used.)

In this dinosaur the adaptations that so characterized *Allosaurus* of late Jurassic age are carried to an extreme. The skeleton is larger, the skull is relatively larger, the hind limbs are perhaps longer and stronger, and the fore limbs are surprisingly smaller, there being but two functional fingers terminating in small claws. Evidently the forces of predation in *Albertosaurus* were concentrated in the large jaws, armed with strong, dagger-like teeth. This dinosaur probably could run fast enough, in a ponderous manner, to overtake its prey, which it would dispatch with the jaws and large, clawed hind feet. It was probably also a carrion eater. One can wonder as to how the ridiculously small fore limbs and

Tyrannosaurus about to attack the hadrosaur *Anatosaurus*. The duck-billed dinosaur would have been virtually help-less against such an enemy; its only hope of safety would have been to escape into water where it could swim away. In the background are ostrich dinosaurs of the genus *Struthiomimus*.

The Mongolian dinosaur *Tarbosaurus* was closely related to the late Cretaceous carnosaurs of North America, particularly to *Tyrannosaurus*. Its adaptations are indeed very close to those of *Tyrannosaurus;* powerful hind limbs, remarkably small fore limbs, a long tail useful for balance, and a huge skull armed with large, blade-like teeth.

Dromiceiomimus, shown within a late Cretaceous redwood forest in what is now Alberta, was one of the agile ostrich dinosaurs. These coelurosaurs, about the size of a modern ostrich, were in many respects remarkably similar to the large ground birds of today, even to the lack of teeth and the development of the jaws as a bird-like beak. This evolutionary development among the ostrich dinosaurs indicates a manner of life parallel to that of modern ostriches.

two-fingered hands were used. It has been suggested that in such a dinosaur the fore limbs were used as props to push against the ground when the animal was lying down on its belly, thereby enabling it to raise the body when the hind limbs were straightened from a folded position. This argument maintains that without such assistance from the fore limbs the action of the hind limbs would merely slide the body along the ground. Perhaps.

To digress, the features that distinguish *Albertosaurus* are carried to even greater extremes in *Tyrannosaurus*, which lived at the very end of Cretaceous time. *Tyrannosaurus*, the greatest of all carnivorous dinosaurs, is even larger than *Albertosaurus*, the skeleton being some forty feet in length. The skull is huge, giving a great gape to the jaws, the tail is long in part as a counterbalance, the hind limbs are very heavy for the support of so large an animal, and the fore limbs are extraordinarily small.

A very close relative of *Tyrannosaurus* is *Tarbosaurus*, found in the Upper Cretaceous beds of Mongolia. Another large carnosaur is *Spinosaurus* from the Upper Cretaceous sediments of Egypt, distinguished by a large sail on the back—perhaps a temperature-regulating device.

Returning to the Oldman fauna, there are in this assemblage some lightly built theropod dinosaurs, about the size of modern ostriches and often designated as "ostrich-dinosaurs." *Struthiomimus* (*struthion*, ostrich; *mimos*, mimic) is an Oldman genus. In this dinosaur descended from coelurosaurian ancestors, the hind limbs and the feet are long and slender—an indication of great running speed. The fore limbs also are long and slender, but obviously were not used for locomotion; rather they were efficient arms and hands for grasping and holding objects. The neck is long and flexible and the skull is small. An interesting feature of the skull is its lack of teeth; the upper and lower jaws form a long beak, and in life probably had a horny covering. The resemblance of *Struthiomimus* to a modern ostrich (except for a long tail and a lack of feathers in the dinosaur) is uncanny; it is a nice example of convergent evolution, of unrelated animals becoming adapted for a similar mode of life. One may reasonably think that *Struthiomimus* lived as do modern ostriches, running across the land at great speed,

catching small reptiles, and probably eating fruits and other plants as well.

Such dinosaurs evidently were very successful; they are found in very late Cretaceous beds in North America and Mongolia. They all look very much alike.

From the Nemegt beds of Mongolia there has been found the fore limbs and hands (and that is all) of a carnivorous dinosaur named *Deinocheirus* that must have been of monstrous size. These fore limbs are about eight feet long, and the hands end in gigantic claws. One can only speculate about the size of the dinosaur to which they belonged. Someday we may hope it will be found.

At the other extreme, there are some small carnivorous dinosaurs of late Cretaceous age—the Oldman representative being *Dromaeosaurus*. This little dinosaur, about six feet long, is related to *Deinonychus*, the early Cretaceous dinosaur that we met on a previous page. Like its earlier relative, *Dromaeosaurus* has a large, sickle-like claw on the inner toe of the foot. Some close cousins of *Dromaeosaurus* are *Velociraptor* and *Saurornithoides* from the Djadochta beds of Mongolia, the same sediments that have yielded such a fine array of the ancestral horned dinosaur, *Protoceratops*. An amazing discovery, made in 1971, revealed a skeleton of *Velociraptor* associated with one of *Protoceratops*. The two skeletons were in their death poses, with the hands of *Velociraptor* grasping the skull of *Protoceratops* and the sickle claw of the foot positioned as if to tear into the body of *Protoceratops*. It would appear that *Protoceratops*, in turn, had buried its beak within the body of *Velociraptor*. The two antagonists seemingly had killed each other and died, locked together.

The dromaeosaurs, as these several small dinosaurs may be called, are noteworthy because the brain is much larger in relation to body size than is the case among any other dinosaurs. In fact, the ratio of brain to body in these dinosaurs is about six times that of modern crocodiles. It has been suggested that they were blessed with an intellectual capacity quite undinosaurian in its potentialities.

Our main concern so far has been with the dinosaurs of the Oldman Formation as they exemplify in a general way the dinosaurs of late Cretaceous age, with, however, some diversions to look at related non-Oldman dinosaurs. What about the other

Above: A Polish expedition working in the Cretaceous beds of Mongolia discovered the interlocked skeletons of the ancestral ceratopsian *Protoceratops* and a small carnivore *Velociraptor.* It would appear as if these two dinosaurs had died together while fighting—*Protoceratops* perhaps defending a nest, *Velociraptor* perhaps trying to rob the nest of its eggs.
Facing page: A diagram of the *Protoceratops* skeleton (left) and the *Velociraptor* skeleton (right) seen in the photograph above.

animals that lived with the dinosaurs of late Cretaceous age?

As in the case of the Morrison fauna, previously reviewed, there were various backboned animals that have left descendants in our modern world. Thus amphibians and such reptiles as turtles, lizards, and crocodiles lived in Oldman time. Snakes, the descendants of lizards, had now appeared. And in the skies there were flying reptiles, some of gigantic size, and birds of modern aspect. Finally

there were mammals, more numerous than in previous ages, and some representing the ancestors of mammals that inhabit our modern world. There were marsupials, primitive in some respects but none the less very successful mammals. And there were insectivores, the ultimate ancestors of all of the advanced, placental mammals that people the world today.

The dinosaurs that lived in what is now Alberta, and represented by the fossils of the Oldman For-mation, enjoyed a world in which they were dominant. They lived in landscapes of modern aspect, and there seemed to be nothing to challenge their supremacy. Yet beneath their feet and in the sky were the animals that within a few million years were to inherit the earth—frogs and other amphibians; turtles, lizards, and crocodilians; birds; and the warm-blooded mammals, as yet small and insignificant, but with potentialities almost beyond the imagination.

Edaphosaurus, a Permian reptile (not a dinosaur), illustrates the "sprawling" posture seen in primitive reptiles.

TO WALK, TO RUN, TO LEAP

There is a great deal more to becoming a giant than merely growing from something little into something big. And there was a great deal more to becoming a dinosaur than the mere transformation from a small, primitive reptile to a large, very specialized reptile. Not that all of the dinosaurs were giants, or even large, but the trend toward great size was very pervasive during the diverse evolution of the dinosaurs, and must be taken into account. Whether large or small, the dinosaurs became what they were because of their immediate heritage from Triassic thecodont reptiles, and a central fact of that heritage was pose.

One might not think that the mere stance an animal takes, its natural pose, would loom large in determining its evolutionary fate, but such was the case with the dinosaurs. A basic character that set the dinosaurs apart from almost all other reptiles was their upright pose—their ability to stand with the feet well beneath the body and close to a midline under the animal. This very important way of standing and walking and running, perhaps as cru-

The dinosaurs were notably "upright" reptiles, standing (as seen in *Styracosaurus*) with the feet well beneath the body and the body raised above the ground. Such a posture would have facilitated an active mode of life.

cial as anything in making the dinosaurs what they were, was a direct inheritance from their thecodont ancestors.

The first reptiles, and even all but the most advanced mammal-like reptiles of Permian age, were essentially sprawling animals moving across the ground in a clumsy manner, supporting their bodies on four short limbs, with the elbows strongly everted to the sides, with the knees perhaps less so. It was not an especially efficient way in which to walk, in part because the body was slung between the spread-out legs, causing a great deal of strain on bones and muscles. One may see it today in the gait of a giant Komodo lizard; this reptile walks with the body raised off the ground, but walking is not at all graceful, and it does not seem to be easy.

With the appearance of the early thecodont archosaurs, at the beginning of Triassic time a new method of locomotion was introduced among the four-footed animals, a method whereby the feet were drawn in beneath the body so that the limbs were working with rather than against the force of gravity. This was especially apparent among some of the small thecodonts known as pseudosuchians, many of which quickly became adapted for walking and running on their hind limbs, much as do birds, with the fore limbs free for the gathering of food.

Here we see the heritage of the dinosaurs.

It has been argued that all of the dinosaurs were eventually descended from bipedal ancestors, from little pseudosuchian reptiles nicely adapted for running on their hind legs, and although this viewpoint has been challenged by some, there is no doubting the fact that the early Triassic dinosaurs were bi-

A late Jurassic confrontation. The giant carnivore *Allosaurus* meets a turtle. Dinosaurs, active and aggressive, were in time to disappear; turtles, slow and meek, were to continue so that their likes are still with us.

Three-toed dinosaur footprints on an Upper Triassic rock surface in the Connecticut Valley. This illustrates the bird-like structure of the feet in the early dinosaurs.

pedal reptiles. They made narrow trackways as they ran, with the left and right hind feet almost but not quite in line. It was a good way to run; it kept the lines of force moving in a forward direction and it eliminated much of the lateral sway that had made walking and running a strenuous exercise for many early reptiles.

From such an ancestry the dinosaurs evolved as efficient walkers, whether they were large or small. It was a particularly efficient method of locomotion for the great giants, the immense sauropods. The gigantic footprints from Texas, shown on page 146, each as large as a washtub, prove quite conclusively that these reptiles walked with the right and left feet close to a midline, just as do elephants today. Such a stance allows gravitational forces to pass down through the heavy limbs, thus reducing the expenditure of energy to a minimum.

Since we are land-living animals we are perhaps prone to forget how much of our energy is devoted to the fight against gravity. For a giant animal this battle is long and unending, and for some relief may be found by taking to the water, by transferring to an environment where the body is supported so that the animal becomes essentially weightless. We know that some of the dinosaurs did this, among them the sauropods. There is a fascinating series of footprints found near Bandera, Texas, showing how a group of twenty-three sauropods traveled in a herd, the smaller ones in the middle, protected by the large adults along the flanks. In the water the smaller dinosaurs evidently had to swim, but the adults "poled" themselves along with their front feet, evidently holding the hind legs up, clear of the bottom. The trackways show imprints made by the front feet on what was the bottom of a lake or a similar body of water with seldom an indication of prints by the hind feet, except where animals changed direction and put the hind feet down to accomplish this maneuver.

The large dinosaurs possess various skeletal structures that were important, often necessary, for living as terrestrial giants. Continuing with the sauropods, these dinosaurs have what might be called a sort of Plimsoll line along the body, just at the base of the vertebrae. Below this line the bones of the girdles and limbs are heavy and dense, admirably fitted for the support of great weight; above

One might think of the gigantic sauropod dinosaurs as having a Plimsoll line running along the base of the vertebrae between the shoulders and hips. The vertebrae above this line are remarkably open and light; below it the leg bones and ribs are dense and heavy.

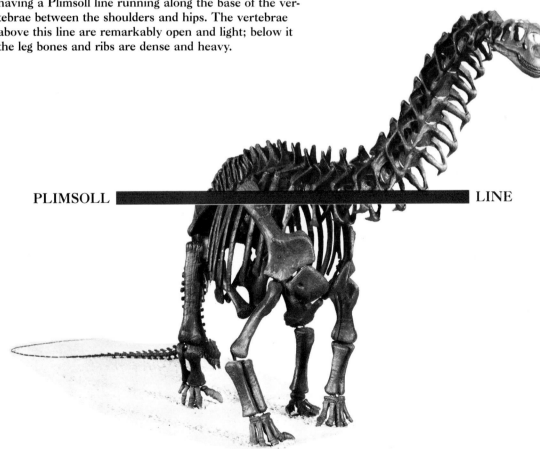

PLIMSOLL LINE

this line the vertebral bones are remarkably light, as has been previously mentioned, with extensive open spaces in areas where bone is not needed. Yet the vertebral column must of necessity be very strong to have supported the weight of the internal organs, so we find that there are extra vertebral articulations to give added strength to the flexible spinal column. The development of a trough along the top of the neck vertebrae, to allow for a strong cable-like ligament for support and control of the head and neck has already been described.

The giant bipedal dinosaurs, the big meat-eating carnosaurs and the hadrosaurs, were faced with the problem of supporting a body weighing many tons on just two crucial side by side pivots—the articulations of the hind limbs with the pelvis. Support was augmented by the incorporation of extra vertebrae into the sacrum so that there was a long connection between pelvis and backbone. So instead of two or three vertebrae in the sacrum, as is common among

reptiles, there may be as many as eight such vertebrae, in *Tyrannosaurus* for example, thereby distributing the strain along an extended and very strong connection.

The support of a giant body on the pelvic pivots was facilitated by the development of a long, strong tail. Not only did the tail constitute a counterbalance to the weight of the body, as for instance it does in modern kangaroos, but also the base of the heavy tail was the anchor for strong muscles that gave power and direction to the hind limbs.

A strong sacral expansion is seen among the armored dinosaurs, where the weight of the armor must have imposed a heavy strain on the pelvis. Indeed, the whole pelvic structure in these dinosaurs is firmly fused to the overlying armor plate.

The problem of weight and size extends to the skull in the giant carnivorous dinosaurs, as we have seen. The skull of *Tyrannosaurus* must have been remarkably light in life (discounting the weight of

The skeleton of *Tyrannosaurus* is nicely engineered for an active animal that weighed many tons and walked on its hind limbs.

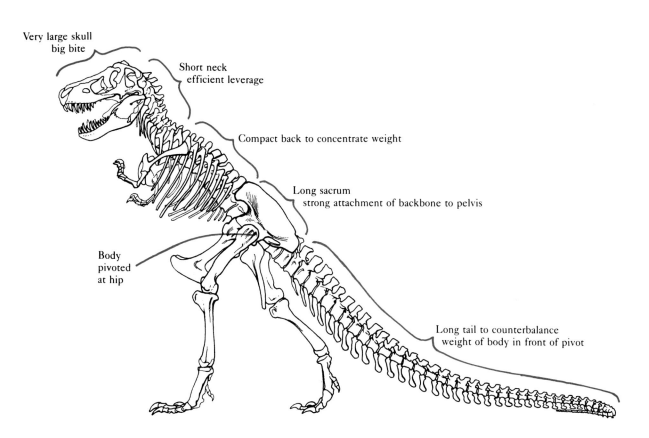

Very large skull
big bite

Short neck
efficient leverage

Compact back to concentrate weight

Long sacrum
strong attachment of backbone to pelvis

Body
pivoted
at hip

Long tail to counterbalance
weight of body in front of pivot

Early dinosaur trackways in Arizona. Note the similarity to the Connecticut Valley tracks—one indication of the wide distribution of dinosaurs during the early years of their evolutionary history. The paleontologist is the late R. T. Bird, a famous dinosaur collector for the American Museum of Natural History, New York.

the jaw muscles), a necessity to make it manageable for quick, vicious strikes against prey and adversaries. Of course, as also mentioned, the neck is composed of short but powerful vertebrae, forming the type of lever needed for such a big skull. Furthermore, the back of the skull of *Tyrannosaurus* is expanded, to furnish a large area for the attachment of powerful neck muscles. It is interesting to see here parallels with modern elephants, which have enormous skulls. The skull of an elephant is surprisingly light, for it contains great sinus cavities above the brain; the neck is short and very strong, and the back of the skull is greatly expanded, affording large areas for the insertions of the powerful neck muscles.

There have been over the years various and sometimes contrasting visions of the dinosaurs as living, moving animals. Some earlier students thought of the dinosaurs, at least the giant dinosaurs, as slow, sluggish reptiles, going about the business of life in a ponderous manner. In fact, some of the earlier authorities thought that the giant sauropods were too large to support their great weight on the land, that they of necessity had to stay in water deep enough to float the body. The sauropod trackways from Texas, especially a dramatic sequence found at Glen Rose, point up the fallacy of this argument. The other extreme has been taken by some modern students, who in some cases visualize large dinosaurs as galloping across the land with marvelous ease and abandon. The facts probably are not described so simply.

It goes without saying that the small theropod dinosaurs must have been active, rapidly running, and even leaping animals. They were not encumbered by problems of size; moreover some of the trackways show that such dinosaurs did scurry across the ground.

How did the gigantic carnivorous theropods move? They, too, probably could walk and perhaps run at a moderate rate, but their movements must nevertheless have been ponderous. The evidence of trackways indicates that these dinosaurs did not drag their tails on the ground when they were walking or running; rather it seems likely that they held the body, in front of the pelvic pivot, and the tail, behind that pivot, in a more or less horizontal position or at a low angle, so that the tail was clear of the ground.

Within recent years some attempts have been made to calculate the speed at which certain dinosaurs moved, from an analysis of their trackways. As based upon studies of locomotion in various living animals, such as ostriches, horses, elephants, and of course men, it has been possible to establish a relationship between body size (as determined by the height at the hip), length of stride, and speed. By applying the formula for this relationship to the trackways of dinosaurs it has been postulated that the speeds at which these ancient reptiles moved was for the most part not particularly great. It would appear that the fastest gaits were attained by the small running theropods, some of which may have been able to run as rapidly as about ten or twelve miles per hour, or somewhat faster. The trackway made by a large hadrosaurian dinosaur that has been so analyzed seems to indicate that the reptile was walking at a rate of about five miles per hour. How much faster it may have been able to run is a matter of conjecture.

The movements of the gigantic sauropods must have been rather laborious because of the immense weight that had to be shifted with each step. A modern-day elephant moves with majestic grace when it is walking at a normal pace, but when the elephant runs at top speed it has a sort of ambling gait; it cannot get all four feet off the ground at once. There must always be contact with the ground. Certainly the same must have been true for the big sauropods.

At just what size the large dinosaurs shifted from being running animals to ambling animals is a matter for speculation. On the African veldt an elephant, weighing five tons or more, can only amble, but a white rhinoceros, the next largest mammal, with a weight of two tons, can gallop. At some point, between the galloping rhinoceros and the ambling elephant, there is a threshold beyond which a running animal cannot free itself completely from the earth. This threshold is determined in part not only by size but also by limb posture and muscle structure; the rhinoceros is built for running and galloping, the elephant is not. Nevertheless size eventually becomes the crucial factor. And so it was with the dinosaurs.

The sauropods probably were walking and ambling types. The armored dinosaurs also may have moved in much the same manner because of the

weight of their armor. Perhaps the smaller ceratopsians could gallop, but one wonders whether the larger members of this group, such as *Triceratops*, could run in this way. It seems likely that *Triceratops* was a ponderous walker.

As for the bipedal dinosaurs, the large carnosaurs and the hadrosaurs may have been able to walk and to run after a fashion. But it is to be doubted that dinosaurs such as *Tyrannosaurus* or *Anatosaurus* ever managed to have both feet off the ground at the same time; theirs was probably a step-by-step progression, the steps being proportionally long according to the speed at which the dinosaur was moving. It was a different story with the small theropods, which would seem to have been active and rapid runners. They probably did run at such speeds that both feet were at times free of the ground; in other words, they could leap. But it

A running elephant. This illustration shows quite clearly that an elephant, because of its great weight, is unable to lift all four feet from the ground at the same time. The same must have been true for the larger dinosaurs.

Cretaceous dinosaur trackways discovered many years ago in Texas are especially impressive because of their size and abundance. They emphasize the gigantic dimensions and power of the big dinosaurs to a degree that cannot be realized from descriptions or pictures, or perhaps even from skeletons. When the viewer is on the ground, side by side with the big sauropod footprints, he can truly appreciate the massiveness of the animals that once walked across a muddy flat, now turned to rock. The prints of the hind feet are a yard and more across, and are pressed deep into the rock.

Around the edges of such prints are the stony rolls of one-time mud, squeezed up by the pressure of the great feet. The prints of the fore feet are not so large, yet are none the less exciting. Even more exciting is the record shown here of a giant carnivorous dinosaur following the sauropod. Note the three-toed impression of a right hind foot in the lower left-hand corner of the picture. Beyond it is the track of the left foot, then the right foot close to a sauropod track, then the left foot, again the right foot imprinted *within* a sauropod track, and so on.

seems from the nature of the trackways that their running and leaping involved the alternate use of the limbs and feet, running as do ostriches. They did not seem to hop, as do kangaroos.

There are trackways showing that some of the bipedal dinosaurs, particularly the ornithopods, did come down on all fours, which is not surprising.

The trackways from Glen Rose, Texas, shown on the opposite page, recreate for us a few dramatic moments in the lives of two dinosaurs, a gigantic sauropod and a giant carnivorous theropod. The prints are in marly limestones of early Cretaceous age.

The sauropod was walking across a watery flatland, perhaps a little inlet of the sea. The water was deep enough to float the tail (for trackways evidently made on dry land show that the sauropods did drag their massive tails) but not deep enough to come up to the belly and float the animal in any way. This is shown by the fact that the sauropod tracks are very deep, and around their edges are raised rims, formed by the limey mud having been squished up by the weight of the dinosaur. The tracks occur in pairs, a hind footprint is about three feet in length and almost as broad, and shows clear impressions of the three clawed toes. The fore footprints are smaller and show no claw impressions. The big dinosaur was not taking long paces or strides. It is only about four or five feet longitudinally between the heel of one hind foot and the heel of the foot on the opposite side, the pace, and about nine feet from the heel of one hind print to the heel of the same foot ahead, the stride.

Parallel to and even imposed upon this trackway is the trackway made by the giant carnivore. It obviously was following the sauropod, because at places it stepped into the prints that had already been made by the giant. The strides of the carnivore are similar in length to those of the big sauropod. It appears as if the carnivore was in pursuit of the sauropod giant; is it possible that he made an attack?

WERE THEY HOT – OR COLD?

The late Cretaceous duck-billed dinosaur *Saurolophus* on the edge of a brackish-water inlet in what is now Alberta. A long, solid spine extends back from above the eyes in this dinosaur; perhaps it was used for display or for sexual combat.

A picture has been drawn of dinosaurs very much on the move. Some of them, it is contended, walked slowly and with ponderous motions, others ran and even galloped, still others leaped lightly on bird-like feet. However they moved, they would appear to have been active animals.

How could these reptiles, for they assuredly were reptiles, have been as active as is attested by the structure of their bones and by the testament of their footprints? How could cold-blooded animals have wandered so widely across the continents, from equatorial regions to high latitudes? How could such vertebrates establish so completely their dominance on land, through scores of millions of years?

Questions such as these have raised the image of the "hot-blooded dinosaurs." Were the dinosaurs cold-blooded, as are the reptiles of our modern world, and if so, how did they overcome the limitations that go with cold-bloodedness, or were they warm-blooded, or "hot-blooded," as are the birds and mammals of today, thereby having the energy

Even the most active of the dinosaurs must have taken time to rest and relax. The giant carnivore *Albertosaurus* is here shown in an unconventional but thoroughly convincing pose.

to live very active lives? These opposed possibilities have created a scientific debate that today is very much in the public realm. People far and wide seem to be intrigued with the idea of warm-blooded dinosaurs, whether such people are paleontologists or not. It is a matter that deserves attention.

First of all let us make some definitions. In very broad terms "cold-blooded" animals are those that derive their core body temperatures (as distinguished from superficial skin temperatures) from the environment in which they live; such are the fishes, amphibians, and reptiles of our modern world. "Warm-blooded" animals are those that have an internal mechanism for creating and maintaining their core body temperatures independent of environmental temperatures, such are modern birds and mammals. Speaking more properly, the cold-blooded animals are ectothermic–deriving their core body temperatures from without; warm-blooded animals are endothermic—deriving their core body temperatures from within.

To refine these definitions, ectothermy is a *pat-*

tern of temperature regulation depending upon behavior and self-governing gain or loss of environmental heat. Endothermy is a pattern of temperature regulation in which body temperature depends on a high, controlled rate of internal heat production.

Another term, poikilothermy, is the wide variation of body temperature as a proportional function of environmental temperature. It is often used as a synonym of ectothermy, but it is not quite the same. Likewise, the term homeothermy, often used as more or less synonymous with endothermy, is a pattern of internal temperature regulation that maintains body temperature within arbitrarily defined limits.

Continuing, heterothermy is a pattern of temperature regulation in which variations of core temperature exceed the definition of homeothermy. Finally, heliothermy is the regulation of core body temperature by exposure to solar radiation.

With these definitions out of the way, we can now proceed to some consideration of cold-blooded versus hot-blooded dinosaurs, or, if you will, ectothermic versus endothermic dinosaurs.

The arguments that have been brought forward to support the idea of endothermy among the dinosaurs have been based upon several facts and seeming facts, and upon assumptions derived from them. The facts and seeming facts are: the pose of the dinosaurs as based upon anatomical studies, the structure of the bones in dinosaurs, the length of the limbs and the size of the brain in dinosaurs, and the supposed ratios of dinosaurian predators to dinosaurian prey.

The pose or stance characteristic of the dinosaurs has already been discussed, and it has been shown that these reptiles differed from other reptiles in having the limbs brought in beneath the body. Those who favor endothermic dinosaurs argue that such an erect pose is an "endothermic stance" characteristic today of birds and mammals. It is to be contrasted with the sprawling pose of reptiles with which we are familiar, an attitude in which the limbs are extended out from the body, more often than not with the belly usually resting upon the ground. This might be termed the "ectothermic stance" among the land-living backboned animals.

This difference between ectotherms and endotherms among modern terrestrial vertebrates would seem to be valid and invariable, therefore should it not also be valid in separating the dinosaurs from other extinct reptiles? Possibly so, but as has been pointed out by critics of dinosaurian endothermy, no cause and effect relationship between posture and the nature of body temperature can be proven. We can only say that the possible correlation of an erect posture with endothermy in the dinosaurs appears to be valid. It constitutes possible but not probable evidence bearing upon this problem.

In line with this argument it has been maintained that the long limbs of dinosaurs (and the dinosaurs are notably long-limbed reptiles) are an indication of endothermy as contrasted with the more primitive Permian reptiles, which were short-limbed and presumably ectothermic. This is not a strong argument; there are numerous short-limbed endotherms in our modern world, while many living ectotherms, notably various lizards, have long, slender limbs.

Still another argument is based upon the size of the brain in relation to the size of the body. A relatively large brain is a mammalian character, and to a lesser degree a bird character as well, and it would seem to go along with endothermy. Most of the dinosaurs had remarkably small brains, which would point to ectothermy among these reptiles. But some of the later Cretaceous theropod dinosaurs did have very large brains for dinosaurs; it has been mentioned on page 133 that certain dromaeosaurs had brains about six times as large in relation to body size as the brain in modern crocodiles. So perhaps dinosaurs such as these may have been endothermic, even though other larger dinosaurs were not.

The subject of dinosaur brains raises a special problem in which the question of ectothermy versus endothermy is involved, especially among the gigantic sauropod dinosaurs. This has to do with the vertical distance between the heart and the brain, which often would have been as much as fifteen to twenty feet in large sauropods when the head was raised high above the body. Such a pose of the neck would have required high blood pressure at the heart level to overcome the hydrostatic pressure of blood in the carotid artery leading to the brain, and it would seem that to produce such high blood pressure the heart necessarily would have had four chambers as in the modern mammals, not

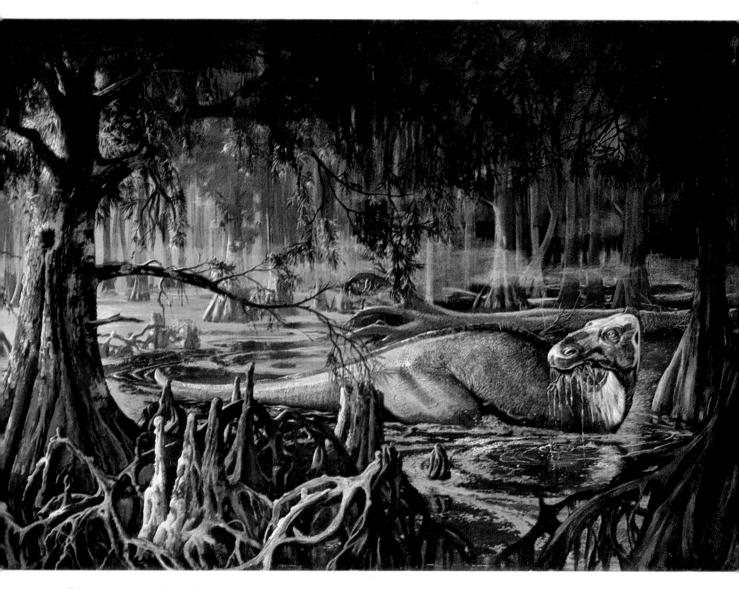

Edmontosaurus, a large late Cretaceous hadrosaur, found in Alberta, in a bald cypress swamp. Fossil plants associated with this dinosaur indicate that it fed upon the leaves of bald cypress and other trees. Perhaps this water-loving dinosaur frequented swamps and rivers not only for protection from giant carnivores but also as a method for controlling its body temperature, as do crocodiles today.

three chambers as in modern reptiles, except crocodiles. Only a four-chambered heart characteristic of endothermic mammals, it is argued, could have produced the pressure necessary to raise the blood through a long, vertical neck to the brain. Could a heart of the ectothermic crocodilian type, which has four chambers but not so nicely arranged as the chambers of the mammalian heart, been sufficient for the task? The question is an open one.

In this connection it may be useful to look briefly at the giraffe, a modern animal (endothermic, it is true) with a neck so long that the head is raised some ten feet above the heart. The blood pressure of a giraffe at heart level is approximately double that of a man, yet when the blood enters the brain it is about equal to human blood pressure. As the carotid artery of the giraffe enters the brain it divides into a network of capillaries known as the *rete mirabile*, and this may help to regulate blood pressure in the brain. Is it possible that the sauropod dinosaurs might have had similar adaptations to regulate the circulation of the blood within a long, sinuous neck?

While speaking of long necks, another question may be considered. Because the long neck of a giraffe encloses a long trachea, or windpipe, there is always a column of dead air within the windpipe that serves no purpose in gas exchange. In order to pull sufficient air into the lungs the giraffe hyperventilates—it breathes faster and more deeply than do mammals with short necks. Yet the oxygen content of arterial blood in the giraffe is not high, rather it is marginal. If a giraffe is taken to a high altitude, where the air is thin, it experiences real distress in breathing. One would suppose that the big sauropod dinosaurs may have had similar problems in breathing—although if they were ectotherms with a low output of energy perhaps such problems were not so critical as in the endothermic giraffe.

Much has been made of the ratio between predators and prey in the world of dinosaurs. In Africa today where natural conditions still prevail, great hosts of herbivorous mammals are preyed upon by comparatively small numbers of predators. Some careful surveys indicate that the predators constitute only a very small percentage of the total animal population in any designated area, generally speaking on the order of one to six percent. In other words, many herbivores are needed to keep one endothermic carnivore alive, a lion, for example, eating its own weight in prey about every eight to nine days. Studies of the large ectothermic Komodo lizard in the East Indies would seem to indicate that it consumes its own weight in prey about every sixty days, thus showing a ratio of predator to prey much lower than in mammals. All of which points up the fact that an endothermic carnivore pays a high price for being warm-blooded.

Some careful surveys made in the late Cretaceous rocks of Alberta, where the Oldman and Edmonton formations are exposed, show a ratio of carnivorous dinosaurs to herbivorous forms of about three to five percent. This has been taken as an indication that the dinosaurs were endothermic, the giant predators requiring a volume of prey intake comparable to what is seen today on the African veldt. But figures such as these are subject to some large possible errors. The accidents of preservation and discovery play a large role in the building up of fossil collections. This in itself introduces a source of error so indeterminate as to make any conclusions based upon predator-prey ratios in fossil collections extremely suspect.

Finally, we come to one type of evidence that would seem to be very persuasive, and this is the microscopic structure of bones in dinosaurs, as compared with bone structure in other reptiles and in mammals. In modern ectothermic reptiles the compact bone of the limbs and other parts of the skeleton show very limited numbers of vascular channels for the accommodation of blood vessels. Bone such as this is called primary vascular bone. In birds and mammals, on the other hand, the compact bone is traversed by numerous vascular channels (of secondary origin), these being the well-known Haversian canals. The presence of the Haversian canals is supposed to be concomitant with endothermy, with the high demand for calcium and phosphorus in animals with high levels of metabolism.

It is interesting that dinosaur bones show a highly vascular system of Haversian canals, very like what is seen in the endothermic birds and mammals. And this would appear to be a strong argument—perhaps the strongest that has been produced—for endothermy in the dinosaurs. Unfortunately there are some problems.

Recent studies show that the presence of Haversian bone is not consistent among living animals. It is present in some ectotherms, such as turtles and crocodiles, and is absent in some endotherms, especially small birds and mammals. Therefore it has been suggested that Haversian bone may be related to such things as rates of growth, or size, or strength of bone, all dominant features among the dinosaurs, rather than to endothermy.

In summary, then, it would seem that all of the arguments that have been advanced to support the concept of warm-blooded dinosaurs are seriously flawed. None is conclusive.

Some further considerations are now in order.

Modern ectotherms are very much the prisoners of their environments. Lizards and snakes, turtles, and crocodiles live by the cycles of day and night,

and of summer and winter. Moreover, they are restricted by the latitudes at which they live. Lizards and snakes, for instance, can live at fairly high latitudes, but they accomplish this by going underground to wait out long, hard winters. During the summer months they may be active by day or by night, depending upon their immediate environments. Desert snakes, for example, often stay underground during the heat of the day (for it is just as fatal for an ectotherm to get too hot as to get too cold) and come out at night to hunt. Turtles may rest during the cool night and then emerge in the early morning to bask—to build up body heat by exposing themselves to the sun, until they reach a preferred temperature.

Crocodiles, the closest modern relatives of the dinosaurs, are generally too large to wait out a long winter underground, and so they are restricted to tropical and subtropical environments. Indeed, the distributions of modern crocodilians occupy a band around the earth roughly between the tropics of Cancer and Capricorn. Experiments with alligators have shown that these reptiles operate most efficiently when their core body temperatures are at about eighty-six to ninety-four degrees Fahrenheit. Below those temperatures the reptiles become sluggish and finally immobile, eventually to the point of

death. At a core body temperature of one hundred degrees Fahrenheit, the alligator will die of overheating. Thus alligators and their relatives are severely restricted—by latitudes and by daily temperatures—in spite of which they have been remarkably successful reptiles, living abundantly on the earth since the very beginnings of the dinosaurs to the present day. It is only the predatory activity of modern man, armed with high-powered guns, that has brought about a decline among the crocodilians.

The experiments with alligators have shown that, as might be expected, large individuals heat up much more slowly when exposed to direct sunlight, and they cool off more slowly than do small individuals. It is a matter of body mass; it takes longer for a large mass to heat up and cool off than is the case with a small mass. This immediately suggests the possibility that the giant dinosaurs, so many, many times greater in mass than the largest crocodiles, must have heated up very slowly and likewise they must have cooled off equally slowly. Indeed, there is reason to think, as based upon the results of the alligator experiments, that it might have taken a great many hours for the body temperature of a large sauropod to have been raised or lowered one degree, assuming such a dinosaur was ectothermic. So it has been suggested that such a

Haversian canals, which are secondary vascular channels developed by the remodeling of bone tissue, and seen here in the toe bone of a large dinosaur, are characteristic of the bones not only of dinosaurs, but also of crocodilians, tortoises, birds, and mammals. It is now thought that the Haversian canals, once considered as indicating endothermy, or "warm-bloodedness," may be related to size, rates of growth, and strength of bone.

Crocodiles and alligators are the closest living relatives of the dinosaurs. Therefore it is logical to think that physiological problems among the crocodilians may afford some clues as to dinosaurian physiology.

About a dozen alligators, ranging from small to rather large individuals, were placed in the sunlight of a summer day in Florida, and their temperatures were taken at frequent intervals. It was known that one hundred degrees Fahrenheit is the crucial core body temperature for these reptiles, at which point the animal succumbs to death. As the alligators individually approached the critical temperature they were removed from the sunlight and placed in the shade.

The temperatures of the small alligators went up very rapidly in the sun, and likewise dropped rapidly when the reptiles were shifted to the shade. The changes were progressively slower as the size of the alligators increased. The temperature of the largest alligator increased slowly, and it still increased for a few minutes after this individual was transferred to the shade; then it began to decline. It was evident that the rate of temperature increase and decrease was directly related to the mass of each animal.

From this experiment it can be inferred that if the giant dinosaurs were ectothermic, like their crocodilian cousins, the rates of temperature fluctuation would have been extremely slow; in other words, it probably would have taken many hours for a dinosaur of thirty or forty tons to have raised or lowered the body temperature by one degree. Therefore such dinosaurs would have had the

physiological advantages of an endothermic, or "warm-blooded," animal without the expenditure of energy so typical of animals that must maintain constant body temperatures. Here is one possible clue to the success of the dinosaurs: it was the conservation of energy.

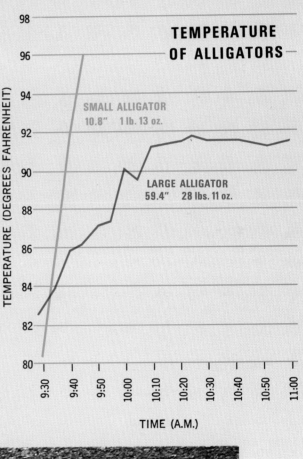

156

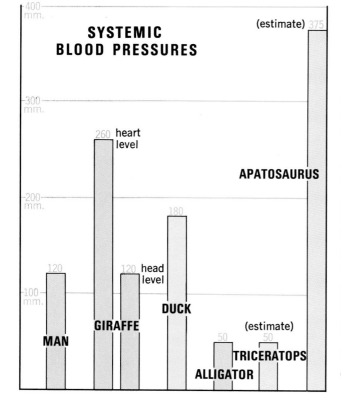

SYSTEMIC
BLOOD PRESSURES

(estimate) 375

APATOSAURUS

260 heart
level

180

120   120 head
                level

DUCK

GIRAFFE

MAN

50   (estimate)
                50

TRICERATOPS

ALLIGATOR

Systemic blood pressures in millimeters of mercury for
man, giraffe, duck, and alligator, and conjectural pressures for two dinosaurs, *Triceratops* and *Apatosaurus.*
Note that in the giraffe the blood pressure is very high
at heart level—about double that of man—a necessity
for pumping blood to the brain, which is far above the
heart. Note also that at the level of the head the blood
pressure is about the same as that for man. By analogy
it is estimated that in *Apatosaurus,* with the head carried
high above the body, the blood pressure may have been
as much as three times that of man. The blood pressure
in *Triceratops,* with the brain only slightly elevated above
the level of the heart, is assumed to have been similar to
that of the alligator—very low.

dinosaur was *inertially homeothermic;* the inertia of
the body mass gave it the attributes of a homeothermic or endothermic animal. Perhaps here is a
partial key to the success of the dinosaurs. The big
dinosaurs, at least, did not need to be warm-blooded in order to have the attributes of a warm-blooded
animal; their immense size made them something
different from the ordinary ectothermic reptile.

But what about the little sauropod, just out of the
egg, and growing up? If these dinosaurs were ectothermic, then it seems reasonable to suppose that
they adopted behavior patterns to control their
body temperatures similar to those seen in modern
lizards, for example. Perhaps they went into the
shade or in the water for protection against excessive heat during the daytime; perhaps they came
out into the sun after a cool night to build up their
body temperatures. In time, when they reached the
status of half-grown sauropods, of dinosaurian
"teen-agers," their body temperatures began to sta-
bilize, owing to their increasing size, so that they
could adopt the life styles of their parents.

These remarks have been concerned with sauropods, but such considerations may be applied to all
of the larger dinosaurs—the dinosaurs that as adults
reached weights of two or three tons or more.

Another point that should be considered here is
the relationship of mass to body surface. The giant
dinosaurs, if ectothermic, gained and lost heat more
slowly than small dinosaurs because of their greater
mass to be heated and cooled; they also retained
core body temperatures more efficiently than small
dinosaurs because of the proportionately less body
surface that allowed the escape of heat from the
body. This, of course, contributed to an inertially
homeothermic condition.

It is all a matter of simple physical laws. As an
object, say a dinosaur, increases in length, the mass
is increased more or less as the cube of the length,
but the surface area is increased at a lesser rate. For
instance, let's look at a cube with a dimension of
one on each edge, and a mass of one (mass being
length times breadth times depth, $1 \times 1 \times 1 = 1$).
The surface area would be six, since there are six
sides (length times breadth of one side times six
sides, $1 \times 1 \times 6 = 6$). If the cube is doubled in
linear dimensions, the mass is increased *eightfold*
($2 \times 2 \times 2 = 8$, compared to 1), while the surface
area is increased only *fourfold* ($2 \times 2 \times 6 = 24$,

Diplodocus from the Upper Jurassic Morrison Formation,
as restored by the eminent artist Charles R. Knight.

Small mass relative to surface

Large mass relative to body surface

Small mass relative to surface

In the sauropod dinosaurs the huge body and upper parts of the limbs had comparatively small surface areas in relation to mass, while the neck, tail, and lower limbs had comparatively large surface areas in relation to mass. Perhaps the long, slender neck and tail and the lower limbs were regions for the rapid assimilation and dispersal of heat, and therefore were important in the regulation of body temperature.

compared to 6, the surface area of the original cube).

Of course an animal is not a cube, but the principle holds. With increase in size there is a proportionately greater increase in mass than in surface area, hence there is greater conservation of heat in the larger animal. And this can turn into a problem for a very large animal. For example, elephants have very large ears, which serve as surfaces for the dissipation of excess body heat; there is method behind the fanning back and forth of the great ears of an African elephant. Giant whales have extraordinarily small areas of body surface in relation to mass, and this, combined with their thick layers of fat or blubber, enables them to live comfortably in polar waters.

The giant dinosaurs probably did not have layers of fat, nor did they have insulating hair, as we know from the fossilized skin of dinosaur mummies, but they may have had problems of heat retention. They could not afford to get too hot, and for them one solution to this problem would have been to seek the shade of large trees, or in the case of the sauropods, to go into the water and submerge themselves. Perhaps, however, the long, slender necks and the long tails of the sauropods would have aided in heat control, for these parts of the body would have had comparatively large areas of skin surface relative to their mass.

It has been suggested that other giant dinosaurs had other strategies for control of body temperatures. For example, the large plates of the stegosaurs show that they probably contained extensive blood vessels; therefore it has been postulated that these were radiators, for the absorption of solar heat when necessary and the dissipation of body heat when necessary. Furthermore, according to this theory, the alternate arrangement of the plates would have been advantageous for such functions.

The great frills of the horned dinosaurs may also have served in part as surfaces for temperature control.

One of the large plates from the back of *Stegosaurus*. Note the deep vertical grooves on the surface of the plate, seemingly to house large blood vessels for the absorption of solar heat and the dissipation of excess body heat. In other words the plates of this late Jurassic dinosaur may have been radiators for temperature control.

But what about other giant dinosaurs, the armored dinosaurs and the hadrosaurs, which lack any such special structures? Perhaps the armored dinosaurs lived such sluggish lives that they did not create temperature problems for themselves as would have more active reptiles. Perhaps the armor made an insulating layer that protected these dinosaurs from excessive solar radiation and at the same time retained core body temperatures, to make the ankylosaurs rather efficient inertial homeotherms. As for the hadrosaurs, they may have retreated to deep water as they felt their body temperatures rise, just as crocodiles do today. The great carnosaurs may have sought the shade, or even have gone into the water as well. Recent evidence indicates that some of these dinosaurs, at least, were able to swim.

In summary, it would seem that there was no overriding need for the giant dinosaurs to have been endothermic in order to have led the very active lives that seemingly many of them did. Their inertial homeothermy sufficed to allow them the advantages of relatively constant body temperatures at an optimum level.

Indeed, there is reason to think that such a strategy would have been more efficient for these dinosaurs than if they were endothermic. As we have seen there is a high cost in being endothermic, the cost of maintaining a high and relatively constant body metabolism, this in turn requiring a large amount of food intake. For giant animals living in regions with year-round equable climates there would have been more conservation of energy in living an ectothermic (but inertial homeothermic) type of life than in being an endotherm.

A large elephant weighing five tons or more requires about six hundred pounds of forage a day in the wild.. This is not excessive in view of the size of the animal—only perhaps six percent of its body weight. (Very small endotherms, such as mice and shrews, will consume daily amounts of food equal to or exceeding their body weights — a result in part of energy loss in animals that have very high ratios of body surface to mass.) By extrapolating to dinosaurs the figures for the weight of food consumed daily to body weight in elephants, it would appear that a large endothermic sauropod, such as a forty-ton brontosaur, might require a ton of forage per day. One wonders if such

a vast amount of herbage could be taken in through the small sauropod mouth during the course of twenty-four hours.

It seems more logical to think that a dinosaur like this was an ectotherm, thereby requiring much less food for its daily needs. A modern ectothermic Galapagos tortoise, weighing about three hundred pounds, will eat about ten pounds of food a day, or a bit more than three percent of its body weight. On the basis of such a comparison, the brontosaur might have required no more than a thousand pounds of food a day—perhaps less. This still seems like a lot, but is perhaps within the realm of possibility. Smaller amounts of food intake for other giant dinosaurs, supposing them to have been ectothermic, seem more realistic than the postulation of the amounts that would have been required by endothermic giants.

If the giant and even moderately large dinosaurs were ectothermic, what of the small dinosaurs, particularly the coelurosaurs? Here an argument for warm-bloodedness would seem to have some degree of logic. These were active dinosaurs—as we know from their trackways, and as can be surmised from their skeletal structure. Were they, then, independently endothermic, independent of the other dinosaurs and independent of birds and mammals? In this regard there is good evidence for supposing that the first birds, such as *Archaeopteryx* from the Upper Jurassic limestones of Germany, were derived from coelurosaurian ancestors. Indeed, the line separating a coelurosaur such as *Compsognathus* from *Archaeopteryx* is not a very heavy line, and one may imagine these two as having had a common ancestor at no very great distance in their past histories. If such were the case perhaps the small coelurosaurian dinosaurs *were* endothermic, and passed their warm-bloodedness on to the first birds. Or, of course, perhaps endothermy did not appear prior to the advent of the birds. You can take your choice.

We know that *Archaeopteryx* was a bird, because in the fine-grained limestones in which the several skeletons of this ancestral bird are preserved there are the beautiful imprints of its feathers. (If the fossil feathers had not been present, *Archaeopteryx* very probably would have been classified as a reptile.) Feathers are insulators, which is good reason to think that *Archaeopteryx* was endothermic. If the coelurosaurian dinosaurs were endothermic did they have any sort of insulating coats to conserve body heat? Some students have maintained that perhaps they were feathered, but there is no paleontological evidence for this view.

So the question as to whether the small dinosaurs were endothermic or ectothermic is very much an open question.

It must be admitted that everything that has been said in this chapter is remarkably equivocal. Many lines of evidence and the arguments derived therefrom show that the dinosaurs were warm-blooded—or were not. Perhaps some of the dinosaurs were warm-blooded and others were not. Nothing truly definite can be adduced from the bones and the footprints that are ours to study, and it seems likely that nothing ever will be forthcoming to settle this problem once and for all. The question remains open and seemingly will remain open through the forseeable future. If only a few dinosaurs had survived into modern times!

Overleaf: *Compsognathus*, of late Jurassic age and one of the smallest of the dinosaurs, was found in the lithographic limestones of Solnhofen, Germany. *Archaeopteryx*, the first bird, was found in these same sediments.

If the imprints of the feathers of *Archaeopteryx* had not been found with the skeleton, this bird (a bird because it had feathers) would possibly have been classified as a reptile, perhaps as a dinosaur. The features of the skeleton in *Archaeopteryx* are so very similar to the features of the skeleton of *Compsognathus* that some paleontologists believe the first birds were descended from small theropod dinosaurs.

Such a presumed relationship raises some interesting questions. Was *Compsognathus* endothermic, or "warm-blooded," or did this character, so typical of the birds, become established only with the appearance of feathers? There is good reason to think that feathers originally were for insulation, to help maintain a constant body temperature. Only later, it is thought, did feathers become adapted as wing surfaces, enabling the birds to fly.

BRAINS AND BEHAVIOR

Some remarks have been made on a preceding page about dinosaur brains, which may lead the reader to wonder how we can know anything about dinosaur brains, for certainly the brains of living dinosaurs were relatively soft and incapable of being fossilized. The answer to such a query is that what we know about dinosaur brains is derived from studies of the cranium—the bony house for the brain, located in the back of the skull. It is possible to make casts of the inside of the cranium—endocranial casts they are called—and from these to get some idea of what the dinosaurian brain was like.

Endocranial casts of mammals reproduce fairly accurately the size and configuration of the brain that once occupied the cranial capsule; endocranial casts of reptiles are less accurate. This is because

A confrontation between the giant carnivore *Tyrannosaurus* and the horned dinosaur *Triceratops*, as painted by Charles R. Knight. The ceratopsian is shown defending its young, a pattern of behavior not typical of modern reptiles but quite possibly characteristic of this late Cretaceous dinosaur.

The herbivorous dinosaurs were browsers, eating foliage from trees and bushes. There is good evidence that the hadrosaurs often fed upon pine needles; the crested hadrosaur *Parasaurolophus* is shown in what must have been a characteristic browsing posture.

the brain in modern reptiles is separated from the inner walls of the braincase by loose strands of dura mater, the membrane that surrounds the brain, so that there is some considerable space between brain and braincase. Nevertheless by comparing endocranial casts made from dinosaur skulls with similar casts made from crocodile skulls (in which latter instance the volumetric relationship between brain and braincase is known) it is possible to make some reasonably accurate deductions concerning the dinosaur brain.

The dinosaur brain, as interpreted from endocranial casts, was a characteristic reptilian brain, similar in its general aspects to the brain in crocodiles. It

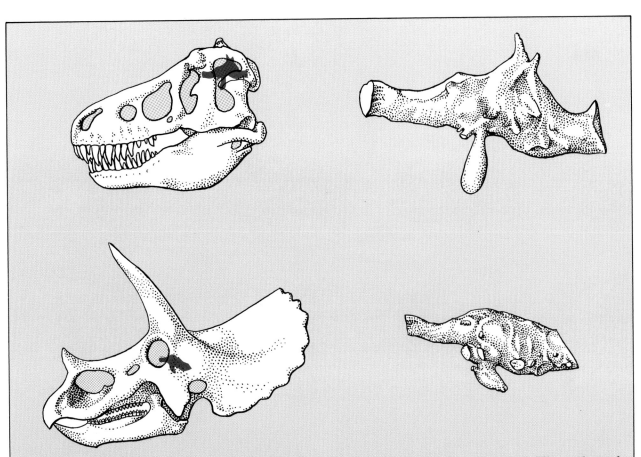

Generally speaking a very large animal has a brain that is *relatively* smaller in comparison to its body size than a small animal. But this does not mean that the large animal is less intelligent than the small animal. The absolute size of the brain is important, as is its structure. The reptilian brain is primitive, with a small forebrain, or cerebrum, yet even among primitive reptilian brains there are differences in size, perhaps implying some differences in intelligence.

Here we see the skull and brain (or rather the endocranial cast) of *Tyrannosaurus* (above), and of *Triceratops* (below). The two skulls are drawn to scale, with the brains to the same scale indi-

cated in their proper positions. The enlarged drawings of the brains on the right are in scale to each other.

Tyrannosaurus must have been more intelligent in a reptilian way than most of the dinosaurs on which it fed. The horned dinosaurs were perhaps more intelligent than many of the other herbivorous dinosaurs, behaving in ways that were comparatively sophisticated for reptiles. Perhaps this was one key to their success in a world where *Tyrannosaurus* and its relatives roamed. However, the brains in any of these dinosaurs were truly small and simple as compared with the brains of large modern mammals, such as elephants.

Two horned dinosaurs of the genus *Pentaceratops* confront each other in a territorial dispute. Each lowers his head, thus displaying the enormous skull frill, in an attempt to drive the other off.

was elongated into a very gentle, horizontal S-like curve, as seen from the side, and the cerebrum (in mammals the "brain proper," which fills most of the cranial cavity) was small and smooth. Such a brain was not that of what we would consider a "thinking animal," and indeed the dinosaurs have frequently been considered as having been stupid, blundering reptiles. Yet the dinosaur brain served these reptiles satisfactorily for more than one hundred million years; during the time they ruled the earth it was sufficiently adequate.

In comparison with their body size, the brain in dinosaurs was generally very small indeed, in a giant sauropod being only .001 percent of the body weight. Only some of the small, active dramaeosaurs had brains of such size that they may be compared with the brains of birds and mammals. But the relative size of the brain, although important, must be viewed in context. Large animals have relatively smaller brains than small animals; the brain-to-body ratio is much less in a dog or a horse than in a mouse, yet all would agree that dogs and horses are probably more intelligent than mice.

Stegosaurus is famous for its tiny brain and for the fact that the enlargement of the spinal nerve cord in the region of the pelvis is some twenty times larger than the brain. For this reason there is a popular notion that *Stegosaurus* had "two sets of brains," which was not at all the case. The brain of *Stegosaurus* must have performed as do all brains, in a very primitive manner of course, while the spinal enlargement, known as the sacral plexus, was an adaptation for control of the large hind limbs and the tail.

As compared with *Stegosaurus* the brain in *Tyrannosaurus* was large, yet when the brain of the giant carnivore is contrasted with the brain of a large mammal of somewhat comparable body size, an elephant for example, it is seen to be very small. *Tyrannosaurus* probably had the ability to behave with more seeming intelligence than *Stegosaurus*, yet even so its actions must have been largely in the sphere of automatic reactions to stimuli. The dinosaurs *were* reptiles, in spite of their differences from other reptiles, and the evidence of the endocranial casts indicates that they probably behaved to a large degree in reptilian ways.

Brains and behavior go together, but there are various clues other than what is seen in the endocranial casts to show how the dinosaurs may have conducted their daily and yearly lives. Since the dinosaurian brain is like the crocodilian brain, one clue is to study the behavior of modern crocodiles. Although modern crocodiles have brains of a lowly sort they are none the less active reptiles that often behave with a certain amount of acumen. They are famous for stalking their prey, floating silently through the waters of rivers or lakes to seize unwary mammals or birds, or lying in wait for animals that come to the shore to drink. They can be terrifyingly aggressive. Yet their aggressive behavior can be at times automatic rather than calculated. For example, alligators are known to be impressed by height rather than by form; thus they may attack a child or a dog or a man sitting on shore, but not a man standing up.

Dinosaurs may have been similarly impressed. It has been suggested, for example, that the great frills of the horned dinosaurs were in part for the purpose of impressing other dinosaurs. A big horned dinosaur would lower the head to charge, thereby raising the frill so that it loomed high like a great shield. Perhaps this impressed an antagonist—another horned dinosaur making a challenge. Perhaps it even impressed attacking carnivorous dinosaurs. It was probably used during sexual or territorial combats; when two ceratopsians had unfriendly encounters, perhaps the one with the larger frill would prevail merely by displaying its frill. The frilled lizard of Australia today employs this very method to frighten an opponent; it has a frill of skin at the back of the head that can be erected to make the animal look larger and more terrifying than it really is.

We know that female crocodilians guard their nests with vicious determination, and when the young are ready to hatch, the mother frequently cracks the eggs with her teeth to help the baby emerge, and then carries the hatchlings to water where they will be safe. Such "unreptilian" behavior very likely was usual among the dinosaurs, and it seems reasonable to suppose that even more sophisticated behavior patterns were present. The discovery of a hadrosaurian "nursery" in Montana has been mentioned.

We need not, however, base all of our comparisons of dinosaurs with crocodilians; there are good reasons to think that the small coelurosaurian dinosaurs and the ornithomimids probably were very

A medieval musician blows through the curved tube of his krumhorne to produce a note that may have been similar to the honking call of *Parasaurolophus*, seventy million years ago. In each case the long tube controls the pitch of the note.

bird-like in their behavior. The resemblance of *Archaeopteryx* to small coelurosaurs points to the probability that bird-like traits, not only in anatomy but also in behavior, were being developed during the transition from reptile to first bird. Furthermore, the remarkable parallelism of the ostrich dinosaurs, such as *Struthiomimus* (even to the development of toothless beaks), to modern ostriches, justifies the assumption that these dinosaurs lived lives very similar to the big ground-dwelling birds of today, the birds we call ratites.

Another aspect of possible dinosaur behavior may be compared with behavior in birds, as well as crocodiles, and this has to do with vocalization. Crocodiles and alligators are noisy reptiles, roaring and bellowing, especially during the mating season, and hissing loudly when they feel threatened. Perhaps dinosaurs were much the same; certainly the structure of the ear in the dinosaurs indicates that they had a very good sense of hearing, and this in turn suggests communication between them. Yet beyond roaring and hissing, some dinosaurs may have had more elaborate forms of making noises; they may have been able to honk and trumpet—one is almost tempted to say perhaps they could sing. These speculations are based upon the elaborate crests in the hollow-crested hadrosaurs, which, as has been suggested, were in part resonating chambers. As has been said the nasal loops in some hadrosaurs have been compared with the loops of a krumhorne, a medieval wind instrument. If the crests were so used, one can imagine the crested hadrosaurs as calling back and forth in deep, resonating tones across thousands of yards, even miles of Cretaceous terrain, signaling to each other as do wolves or coyotes or howler monkeys in our modern world. One may assume that they used their considerable voices to advertise the limits of individual or group territories. It is an interesting subject on which to speculate.

Dinosaurian behavior is often revealed by trackways. The trackways at Glen Rose, Texas, show that a large carnivore was following a sauropod dinosaur. Perhaps the predator just happened to walk along by and in the sauropod tracks, but the close correspondence between the footprints of hunted and hunter leads one to think that here is a record of pursuit and possible attack. The related trackways at Bandera, Texas, show, as described earlier,

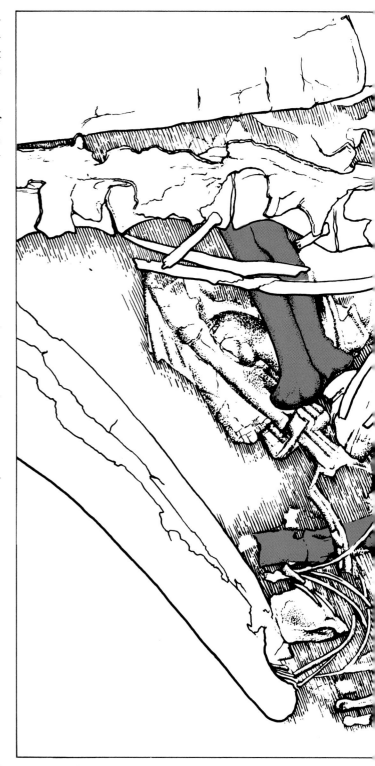

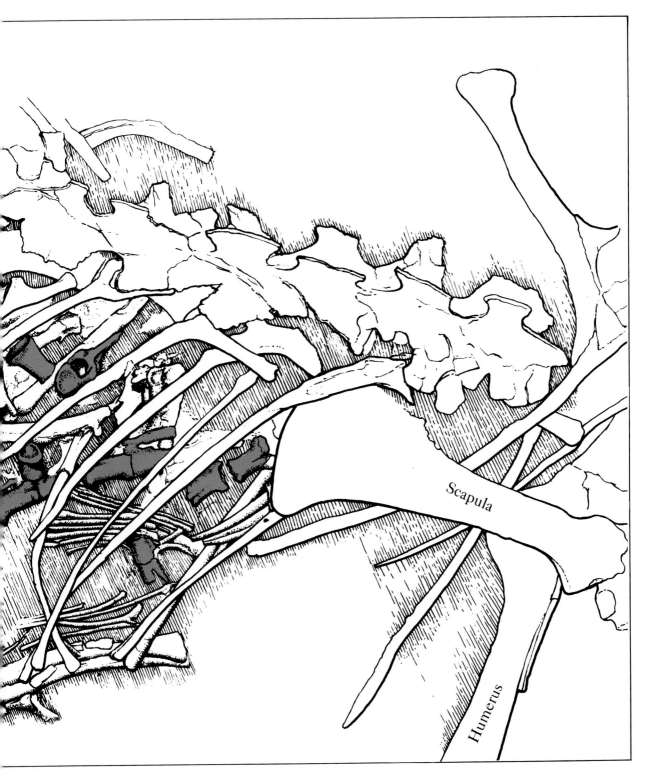

Within the body cavity of this *Coelophysis* skeleton are some limb bones and vertebrae of a young *Coelophysis*, seemingly the remains of a cannibalistic meal.

that a group of sauropod dinosaurs was traveling together, the large adults walking along the outer
edges of the assemblage seemingly to protect the
smaller individuals in the middle. Here is ample
evidence that these dinosaurs were gregarious—
that they moved in herds as do many herbivorous
mammals today. This pattern of living together is
seen among other dinosaurs as well; Triassic footprints at Rocky Hill, Connecticut, have preserved a
record of a large group of dinosaurs walking across a
mud flat near a shore, and the concentrations in

New Mexico of the little Triassic carnivorous dinosaur *Coelophysis* gives evidence of an amazingly
large number of these dinosaurs herding together,
animals of all ages from very small juveniles to
adults. A group of eight skeletons of *Deinonychus*
clustered around a *Tenontosaurus* skeleton would
seem to indicate that these active, highly preda-
ceous carnivores probably hunted in packs.

Such discoveries as that of *Deinonychus* and *Tenontosaurus*, of the little Jurassic coelurosaur *Compsognathus* with a lizard skeleton in its stomach, and of

Pine

Grape

Palm

Poplar

A huge skull of the horned dinosaur *Pentaceratops*, found in the Cretaceous badlands of New Mexico, is literally surrounded by fossilized leaves and stems of plants, affording dramatic evidence not only of the kind of woodland in which this dinosaur lived, but also of what it probably ate. The plants represented by the fossils shown above, together with figs, viburnum, and cottonwoods, furnished the giant herbivore with a varied and ample food supply.

the brontosaur backbone showing toothmarks made by *Allosaurus*, give us glimpses of carnivorous dinosaurs preying upon their victims (or in the case of *Allosaurus* possibly feeding upon carrion) in an ancient world of hunters and hunted. Other discoveries have yielded evidence as to the diets of some giant herbivores, getting their energy directly from plants. Thus, the stomach contents of a hadrosaur mummy show that this dinosaur had eaten seeds, fruits, and pine needles. The striations of hadrosaurian teeth indicate the motions of the jaws as they chewed their food. An especially interesting discovery recently made in New Mexico has revealed a large horned dinosaur, *Pentaceratops*, surrounded by an abundance of fossil plants, showing not only the environment in which this ceratopsian lived, but almost surely the types of plants on which it fed. Included among the plants are fossil leaves of grapes, figs, viburnum, cottonwoods, pines, and palms. We are here afforded a glimpse of a horned dinosaur browsing in a late Cretaceous forest of luxuriant vegetation.

THE LIFE CYCLE

Years ago fossil nests containing eggs were found in association with the small Mongolian ceratopsian *Protoceratops*. Some of the fossil eggs contained embryonic bones. Here the hatching of *Protoceratops* is depicted; tiny dinosaurs are emerging from eight-inch-long eggs.

How long did dinosaurs live? This is a question the answer to which will always be speculative. We can only look at modern animals, and guess.

The dinosaur giants must have had long lives, if for no other reason than that the time required to grow into such massive animals would have been considerable. Of course it might not have taken as long for a dinosaur to grow into a giant as we might think; the long bones of the big dinosaurs showing a marked development of Haversian canals could indicate that growth was rapid in these reptiles. On the other hand the evidence from modern reptiles indicates that even if growth was rapid, the dinosaurs probably were very long-lived animals.

What we know about growth in modern reptiles is at best incomplete, because animals living in zoological parks do not lead "normal" lives, while the study of reptiles in the wild, especially of selected individuals, is extraordinarily difficult. Generally speaking, reptiles do not show a limitation or cessation of growth when becoming adult, as is the case with mammals. In mammals, the epiphyses, or ar-

A nest of *Protoceratops* eggs from the Cretaceous beds of Mongolia. These fossil eggs are in the original positions in which they were found. Note that they are arranged in three concentric circles—an inner circle apparently containing ten eggs, a second circle represented by the three contiguous eggs at the left, and an outer circle indicated by the single egg beyond the nearest of the second-circle eggs. Perhaps this is only a part of what was once a complete nest that may have contained fifty or more eggs.

ticulating ends of the bones, are separated from the main bodies of the bones by cartilage, which allows for growth. As the animal reaches the adult stage these epiphyses become firmly fused to the rest of the bone, so that further growth is not possible. In many reptiles, particularly turtles and crocodiles, such fusion of the epiphyses never becomes complete, so that growth may continue through the entire life of the animal, although at a reduced rate.

Studies of wild alligators indicate that growth of the individual proceeds at about a foot a year for the first ten or twelve years of life. Then it slows down so that the yearly increment is measured in inches rather than feet. The largest of modern crocodilians reach lengths of more than twenty feet; how long it takes to reach such dimensions is not definitely known. (Of course growth rates in these reptiles undoubtedly are affected by environmental conditions—by the number of days per year of optimal temperatures, and by the food supply.) There is good reason, however, to think that crocodilians of such size suggest that an individual eighteen feet in length might well be at least a hundred years old. Larger crocodiles might be considerably past the century mark.

Turtles are notably long-lived reptiles, and some may reach ages of two hundred years or more. There are well-documented records of turtles more than one hundred years in age; a giant tortoise from the Seychelle Islands was captured in the year 1766, was taken to Mauritius, and lived until the year 1918.

How long, then, did the dinosaurs live, especially the giant dinosaurs? One hundred years—very probably; two hundred years—very likely; five hundred years—who knows?

Of course if we compare the giant dinosaurs with large endothermic mammals their estimated ages may not have been so extreme. Endothermic animals burn up energy more rapidly than do the ectotherms; therefore they may have shorter life spans. But since modern elephants, for example, live to be seventy years or more of age, life spans of more than one hundred years for the big dinosaurs do not seem unreasonable.

Alligators, which grow rapidly, reach sexual maturity at about six years of age, at which time they may be about six feet long. It is thought that the Nile crocodile does not attain this adult stage until it is about eight or ten feet in length, and perhaps twenty years of age. It thus seems logical to think that the very small species of dinosaurs may have started laying eggs when they were four or five years of age; that the giants were twenty years or even fifty years old before they began reproducing.

All of the evidence indicates that dinosaurs laid eggs in well-prepared nests, thereby resembling modern crocodiles and alligators. Some modern lizards and snakes are ovoviviparous—that is, the females retain the eggs within the body and give live birth to their young, but there is not any evidence for such a mode of reproduction among the dinosaurs.

The record of dinosaur eggs is well documented, eggs having been found in Mongolia, in southern France, in Portugal, in Africa at the Tendaguru locality, in South America, notably in Brazil, and in western North America, in Montana. In Mongolia and southern France the eggs are abundantly preserved so that our knowledge of them rests upon large samples. And in Mongolia the eggs are found in close association with the dinosaurs to which they belong—the ancestral ceratopsian *Protoceratops*.

In a number of cases nests of dinosaur eggs have been found, the most famous being the *Protoceratops* nests discovered in Mongolia. It is evident that the female dinosaur dug a hole in the sand several feet in diameter and then deposited her eggs in concentric rings within the nest, after which the nest was covered with sand, to be hatched by the heat of the sun. The egg clutches that failed to hatch provide the invaluable evidence as to reproduction in this little dinosaur. Each egg is about eight inches in length and is quite elongated, like the eggs of many modern lizards. The surface of the shell, not leathery as are the eggs of modern reptiles, is rugose and striated by numerous short longitudinal ridges.

The *Protoceratops* nests, of which a considerable number were found in close proximity to each other, may be compared with the nests of the Nile crocodile, also large, circular depressions in the sand, and grouped in what has been called colonial nesting grounds. The crocodile nests, frequently as much as fifteen feet in diameter, may contain as many as ninety eggs, but about fifty is a more usual number. The eggs are deposited in tiers or layers, a

An egg of the Mongolian Cretaceous ceratopsian *Protoceratops,* about natural size. The egg is elongated—similar in shape to the egg of a modern lizard. The shell is rugose; originally it would seem to have been highly calcareous like the egg of a bird, not leathery as are the eggs of modern reptiles.

pattern that may be compared with the concentric rings of eggs in the *Protoceratops* nests.

Not all dinosaur eggs are elongated; some are quite round. Such are the eggs that occur in the same sediments as the bones of the sauropod dinosaur *Hypselosaurus,* in southern France. They are large, some ten inches in diameter, shaped like large grapefruit, and have pebbly surfaces. Eggs of this size are approaching the maximum that can be attained by eggs for there are limits to the strength of egg shell. Moreover, there is no advantage in producing ever thicker shells in order to produce ever larger eggs, because it is necessary for egg shells to be sufficiently thin and porous to transmit oxygen and carbon dioxide between the interior of the egg and the atmosphere.

One wonders if female dinosaurs, after laying their eggs, guarded their nests as do modern crocodilians, or whether they abandoned them to fickle circumstances as do many modern turtles. It is reasonable to think that they did guard the nests, in part because crocodiles and alligators, the closest modern relatives of the dinosaurs, may retain behavior habits that once were common among archosaurian reptiles. The instance of the interlocked skeletons of *Velociraptor,* a small predator, and *Pro-*

toceratops, cited on a previous page, leads to the supposition that perhaps the ceratopsian was defending a nest when it was attacked by the carnivore. It is tempting to believe this. Why not?

There is no doubt that the dinosaurs, since they hatched from eggs, started life as very small reptiles and this applies even to the greatest of the giants. One very interesting discovery of recent years is that of the baby dinosaur skeleton, evidently just out of the egg, shown on page 180. As would be expected, it shows the features that typify baby animals of all kinds, the world over and through time. The head is relatively large, and the eye is very large in relation to the size of the skull. There is a deep, bulbous forehead, and the limbs are short. This tiny skeleton was found in late Triassic beds in Argentina, and it represents a prosauropod dinosaur, the adult of which would have been twenty feet or more in length.

Other baby and juvenile dinosaurs have already been mentioned: the "nursery" of little hadrosaurs in Montana, the sequence of *Coelophysis* skeletons in New Mexico, from very young to adult individuals, and of course the fine age series of *Protoceratops* from egg to adult.

These particular examples are, however, rather

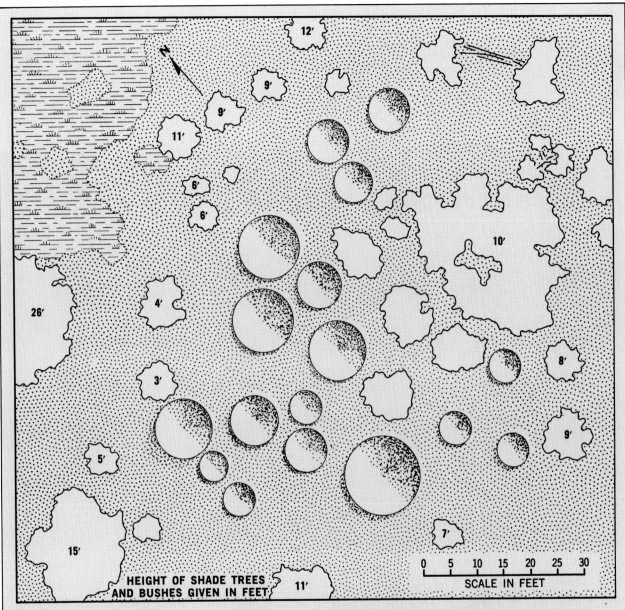

HEIGHT OF SHADE TREES AND BUSHES GIVEN IN FEET

SCALE IN FEET

The Nile crocodile digs its nests in the sand, near a river. Such nests are found in groups, forming communal nesting grounds where these large saurians gather together to start the life cycle of a new generation. Many of the nests are quite large—fifteen feet in diameter, and they are often close together. Some nests may contain as many as eighty eggs arranged in tiers. During the process of egg-laying, sand is shoveled into the nest, so that the eggs, although separated, are packed "like currants in a cake." Some crocodilians, such as alligators, guard the nest during incubation.

Once the eggs are deposited and covered with sand they are incubated by the heat of the sun.

The numerous and contiguous nests containing fossil eggs of the early ceratopsian dinosaur *Protoceratops,* unearthed in Mongolia, indicate that these dinosaurs may have had nesting habits similar to those of the crocodile.

The nests of the Nile crocodile are robbed by the Nile monitor lizard. The discovery of a carnivorous dinosaur, *Velociraptor,* among the *Protoceratops* nests, leads to speculation that here is a record of nest robbing going back millions of years.

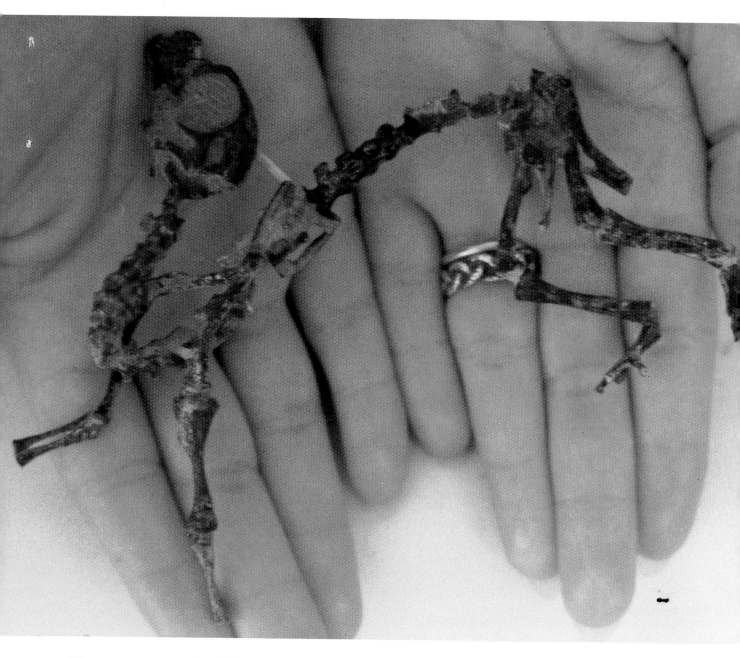

Dinosaurs, no matter what their adult sizes might have been, started life as very small hatchlings. Here is a tiny dinosaur skeleton, just out of the egg—the minute fossil bones of a dinosaur that would have grown up to be as much as twenty feet in length.

The skeleton of a juvenile *Camarasaurus* from the Upper Jurassic Morrison Formation, as displayed at the Carnegie Museum, Pittsburgh. This half-grown sauropod shows some of the characters that might be expected in a young dinosaur of this type—a relatively short neck, a relatively large head, and relatively short limbs.

exceptional. It is a paleontological fact that the remains of young dinosaurs are relatively rare; usually only adults are found as fossils in the rocks. Why should this be? The answer, in part, is that large, heavy bones are more apt to be preserved as fossils than are small, delicate bones. Aside from this it is probable that young dinosaurs lived differently than did the adults. Once more let us look at crocodiles.

Baby crocodiles are liberated from their eggs under the supervision of the guarding mother, and are almost immediately taken in her mouth to nearby water, where they are released. At first they require little food, for a large quantity of egg yolk remains in the body to nourish them for several months. Very quickly the young crocodiles go into seclusion, to remain separated from the adults for several years. Indeed, experienced zoologists and hunters have remarked that after young crocodiles reach a length of a foot or so they vanish, not to reappear

Dromaeosaurus, a small carnivore, scavenging the carcass of the horned dinosaur *Chasmosaurus.* Thus ends the life cycle of a giant; thus the food for life is available to a small meat-eater.

until they have reached lengths of five or six feet. This phenomenon has led observers to remark that one might think young crocodiles to be nonexistent. From studies that it has been possible to make on young crocodiles it is apparent that habits and food preferences are very different in the young than in the adult. The little crocodiles, during their years of isolation, feed first upon insects and crustaceans. Then, as they get progressively larger, they gradually add fishes, reptiles, birds, and mammals. Finally when they have reached the stage of what might be called adolescence, they join the herd.

It may be that this was a pattern among dinosaurs. Perhaps the reason that we seldom find young dinosaurs is because they were living apart from the adults, within environments where they were seldom preserved. Finally, as they came of age they joined the adults, to wander with them and hunt for food with them, as is revealed by the footprints of juvenile and adult sauropods at Bandera, Texas.

Eventually the life cycles of individual dinosaurs

came to an end. Very probably most of them died or were killed long before they had reached extreme old age, as is the rule among wild animals today. Some suffered the trauma of old age. There are examples of dinosaurs in which arthritis was taking its toll, as seen for instance in some deformed tail vertebrae of *Diplodocus*. (Arthritis is a very ancient disease.) Some suffered accidents from which they recovered; healed bones that had been broken are not uncommon among the fossils of dinosaurs. Some,

the very large individuals, probably had approached the limit of their separate roads of life, terminating sojourns on earth that may have stretched through a hundred, or perhaps several hundred years.

Yet before their several demises these dinosaurs had reproduced their own kind. Eggs had been laid and babies had hatched, to continue the lines of dinosaurian evolution that were to dominate the earth for more than a hundred million years.

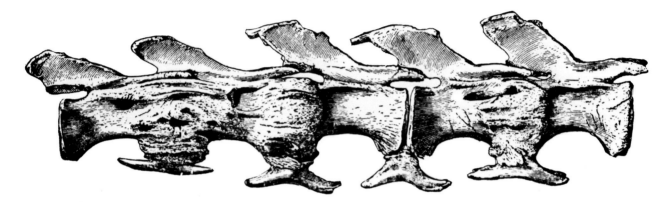

A section from the tail of *Diplodocus* containing five vertebrae, those on the left showing articular lesions caused by arthritis.

THE WORLD IN WHICH THEY LIVED

The fossil bones and footprints of dinosaurs have been found far and wide, on all of the continents except Antarctica, and on such isolated islands as Spitzbergen, far north of the Arctic Circle, and New Zealand, one of the most southerly inhabited lands in our modern world. (Although dinosaurs are not known from Antarctica, abundant fossils have been found there of early Triassic reptiles that lived some millions of years before the appearance of the first dinosaurs. There is still much exploratory work to be carried on in Antarctica, and it is quite possible that the remains of dinosaurs may be found there in future years.) How do we explain the wide and in some cases the disparate distribution of the dinosaurs in the world of today? The answer to this query is that the dinosaurs of yesterday lived in a world unlike the world with which we are familiar.

The late Cretaceous dome-headed dinosaur *Pachycephalosaurus* waiting out a Mesozoic rain storm. The giant gunnera leaves and the other plants dwarf *Pachycephalosaurus*, which was in fact a rather large ornithischian dinosaur.

185

The crust of the earth is divided into a series of great plates, some of them enclosing continents and oceanic areas around the continents, one, the Pacific Plate, containing the basin of the Pacific Ocean. These plates have been in constant motion for millions of years and they are still moving. Some of them are pulling apart, as in the case of the American plates, which by a westward movement are separating from the African and Eurasian plates along a sinuous ridge down the middle of the North and South Atlantic oceans. Others are colliding, as in the case of the American plates grinding against the Pacific Plate.

Where plates pull apart, hot rocks, or magmas, from deep within the earth rise through the cracks that are formed to create oceanic ridges. Such is the mid-Atlantic ridge equally distant between the eastern and western hemispheres, and cutting through the middle of Iceland. Volcanoes are often formed along such ridges, as we have seen in recent years in Iceland.

Where plates collide, one plate descends beneath the other, which overrides the descending plate. Deep oceanic trenches are formed along the zone of subduction, as it is called, and mountains are wrinkled up by the pressures of the colliding plates. Such are the oceanic trenches and the mountain chains along the western borders of the two Americas. Earthquakes are frequent and volcanoes arise in long lines along these colliding borders. The Pacific Basin, which is in collision with other plates around much of its periphery, is surrounded by a volcanic "ring of fire."

Although most of the boundaries between plates are within oceanic basins or along the edges of continents, some of them cut through continental regions. Thus the Indian Plate, which collided with Asia many million years ago, thereby wrinkling up the Himalayan barrier, is bounded on the north by the immense mountain range that separates India from the rest of Asia. And conversely East Africa and Asia Minor are separating from the bulk of the African continent along the Rift Valley and the Red Sea.

Such are the relationships of the continents today. When we journey back through time we see the land masses of the earth becoming ever more closely related, until we reach the end of the Paleozoic Era, when all the land was joined in the immense supercontinent, Pangaea.

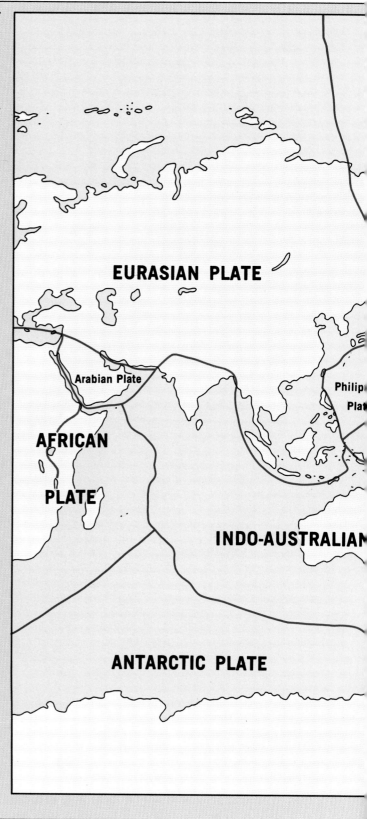

EURASIAN PLATE

Arabian Plate

Philipp
Plat

AFRICAN

PLATE

INDO-AUSTRALIAN

ANTARCTIC PLATE

MAJOR CRUSTAL PLATES OF THE EARTH

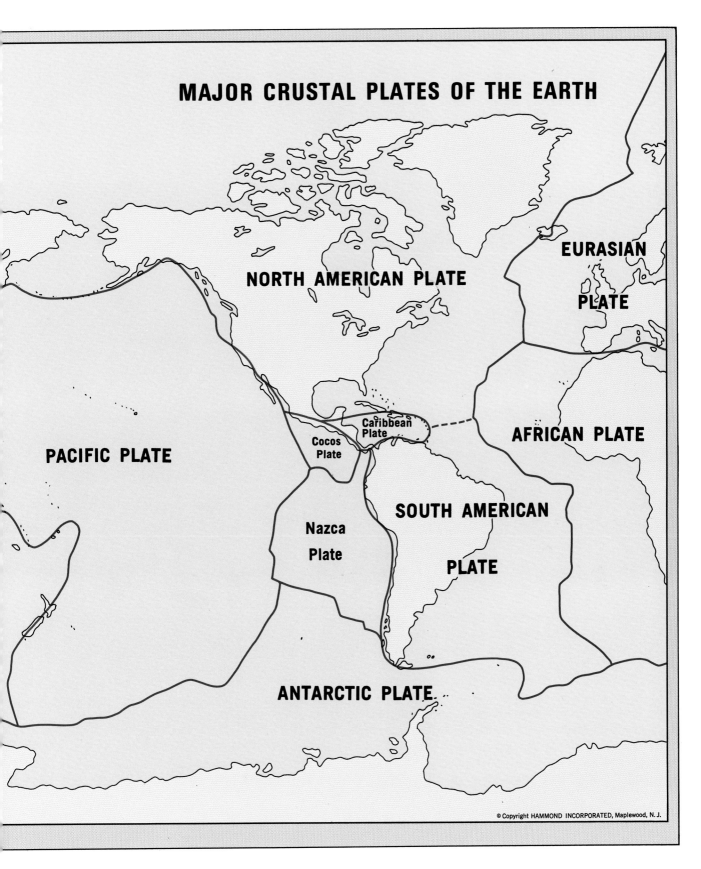

EURASIAN PLATE

NORTH AMERICAN PLATE

AFRICAN PLATE

Caribbean Plate

Cocos Plate

PACIFIC PLATE

SOUTH AMERICAN

Nazca Plate

PLATE

ANTARCTIC PLATE

© Copyright HAMMOND INCORPORATED, Maplewood, N.J.

UPPER TRIASSIC

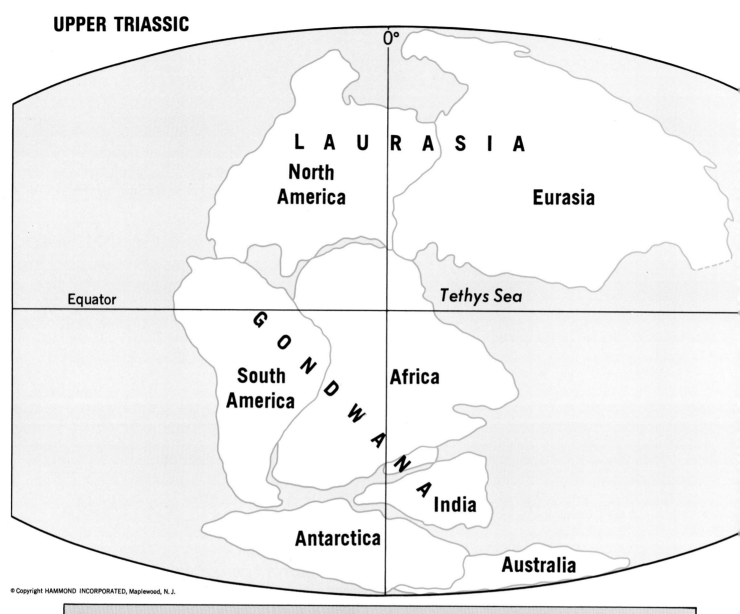

0°

L A U R A S I A

North
America

Eurasia

Equator

Tethys Sea

G O N D W A N A

South
America

Africa

India

Antarctica

Australia

Here is a representation of continental evolution during Mesozoic time. Rifting and the drift of the continents, which had begun during the Triassic Period, proceeded through the Jurassic and Cretaceous periods to a stage where earth's lands began to assume their present forms. Yet during all this time connections were retained between the rifting blocks, so that dinosaurs were able to move rather freely throughout the world.

At the end of the Mesozoic Era South America became an island continent, peninsular India was detached from Africa to begin the rapid movement that resulted in its collision with Asia, North America approached eastern Asia in the Bering region, and Antarctica and Australia, still connected, were closely related to the tip of South America.

With these developments the dinosaurs disappeared, to be replaced on the land by hosts of warm-blooded mammals and birds.

UPPER JURASSIC

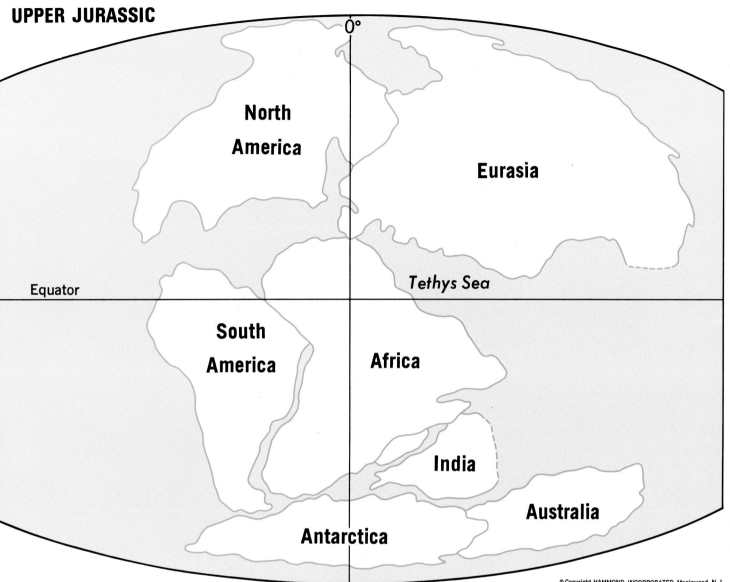

0°

North
America

Eurasia

Equator

Tethys Sea

South
America

Africa

India

Australia

Antarctica

This brings up the subject of plate tectonics and continental drift. Within the past two decades the science of geology has undergone a revolution in thought as profound as the biological revolution initiated by Charles Darwin in 1859. Darwin showed that life has not been static, rather that it has been and is constantly changing and evolving. The new geological revolution, the work of many people rather than a single man, shows that the continents have not been static through time, rather that they have been and are changing in configuration and in their positions.

The idea of drifting continents arose just before World War I, largely as the result of writings by a German meteorologist, Alfred Wegener. At first it did not find favor with most geologists and biologists, but as a result of the development of sophisticated sonar techniques, as well as other disciplines during and after World War II, it became possible to learn much more about the continents and ocean basins than ever before had been known. Indeed, the ocean basins, hitherto hidden beneath the restless waters of the seas, were revealed as though seen through great transparent windows. And it became apparent that these great basins are quite different from the continents; they are not geologically old but rather are of fairly recent development. Moreover it became apparent that the continents have shifted in relation to each other through large distances of latitude and longitude.

UPPER CRETACEOUS

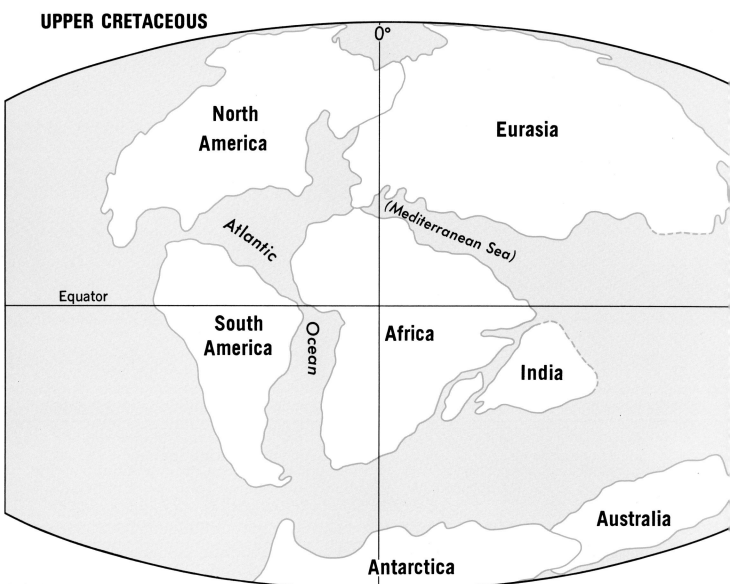

The mechanism for such profound changes in the earth's crust, a mechanism unknown to and undreamed of by Wegener and his contemporaries, has been the constant movement of massive "plates" into which the crust of the earth is divided. These plates, which contain not only the continents but the ocean basins as well, are pulling apart in places, as along the middle of the North and South Atlantic oceans, and colliding in other places, as along the western borders of North and South America. The rifting and collision of the plates mentioned in the above example are the result of the pulling away of the two Americas from original contacts with western Europe and Africa, and their collision with several plates containing the

Pacific Ocean. This magnificent view of the crust of the earth (which incidentally has done much to further our understanding of earthquakes and volcanoes) constitutes the modern theory of plate tectonics, in turn an outgrowth of the older and simpler idea of continental drift. There is a tremendous amount of solid evidence to support plate tectonics—evidence in the fields of geology, geophysics, paleontology, botany, and zoology; plate tectonics is by now so firmly established that it is almost universally accepted.

According to the evidence of plate tectonics there was one great supercontinent, Pangaea, at the time the dinosaurs arose from their thecodont ancestors. Pangaea was in turn composed of two components, a northern portion that has been named Laurasia and consisting of what is now North America and Eurasia minus peninsular India, and a southern part known as Gondwanaland (more properly Gondwana) and consisting of what is now South America, Africa, peninsular India, Australia, and Antarctica. These two land masses were bound together by long contacts between western Europe and northeastern North America, between the eastern boundary of North America and the Mauretanian bulge of Africa, between the western border of Africa and the eastern border of South America, between the southeastern border of Africa and East Antarctica, between Antarctica and the Great Bight of Australia, and between Africa, Antarctica, and peninsular India, this latter mass wedged between the other two. An east-to-west longitudinal sea, the Tethys Sea, terminating in the region of what is now Spain and North Africa, separated the southeast and northeast coasts of Laurasia and Gondwanaland respectively.

In late Triassic time, the years of the first dinosaurs, Laurasia and Gondwanaland were trending toward a separation from each other that involved rotation of Laurasia in relation to Gondwanaland. This was the beginning of the opening of the North Atlantic Ocean and it constricted the Tethys Sea to some extent. But Laurasia and Gondwanaland remained connected at the hinge of rotation, which was the contact between what is now Spain and the northern coast of Africa. During Jurassic time the rifting of the two ancient continents continued, with the North Atlantic becoming wider, yet with the connection at the hinge remaining. The South Atlantic was beginning to open by a very narrow rifting between the southern parts of Africa and South America. Such movements continued through Cretaceous time, with the South Atlantic widening. By the end of the Cretaceous, when the dinosaurs were in the final years of their dominance, South America was breaking away from Africa to drift west, eventually to become an island continent until fairly recent geologic time. Peninsular India was becoming detached from its original position in contact with Africa, to drift to the northeast, eventually to collide with Laurasia, the collision wrinkling up the great Himalayan barrier. Antarctica and Australia, still connected, were beginning the movements that eventually would separate

them, Antarctica drifting to its present position over the South Pole, Australia drifting to the northeast, to assume its position in proximity to southeastern Asia. Finally, North America, although still retaining a connection with what is now western Europe, by reason of a westward, rotational drift, became positioned so that its northwestern region was in close proximity to northeastern Asia, in the Bering region.

In spite of all of these continental movements, during the Mesozoic Era the blocks of land that eventually were to become our modern continents retained enough connections with each other so that there were avenues of communication for the distribution of land animals and plants. This was why the dinosaurs became so widely established throughout the world in which they lived. It was one world, open to the wanderings of active animals, which the dinosaurs were. The fact that the fossils of dinosaurs are now found in such widely separated regions as they are is owing to their transportation, long after burial, on the drifting continents to their present positions. In their days the dinosaurs were living much more closely together than the occurrences of their fossils would suggest.

That is why in Upper Triassic sediments one finds such closely related dinosaurs as *Coelophysis* and *Syntarsus* in western North America and southern Africa respectively. Now they are separated by ten or eleven thousand miles on a great-circle route; then they were within five or six thousand miles of each other—with a broad land connection across which they could move. That is why in sediments of the same age the prosauropod dinosaurs lived across a continuous range, where now their bones are widely separated, in Europe, China, southern Africa, North and South America.

The examples might be continued, to involve dinosaurs of Jurassic and Cretaceous age, but there is no need to give long additional lists. Suffice it to call attention to the close relationships between dinosaurs of the Upper Jurassic Morrison beds in western North America and those of the Tendaguru beds in eastern Africa, or similarly the very close relationships of the Upper Cretaceous dinosaurs of Mongolia and western North America.

It was not only the positions of the lands on which the dinosaurs lived that determined the broad distributions of these reptiles throughout the

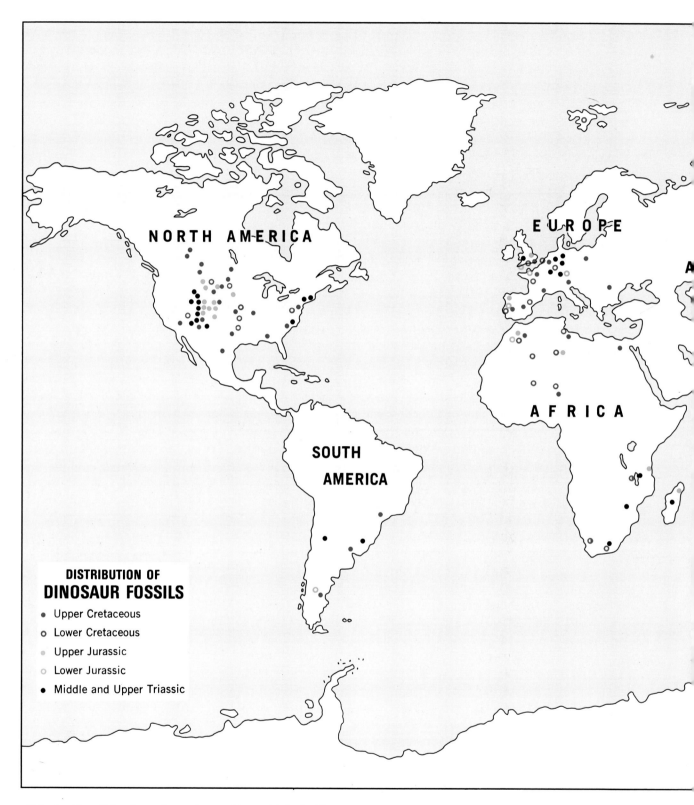

DISTRIBUTION OF DINOSAUR FOSSILS

- Upper Cretaceous
- Lower Cretaceous
- Upper Jurassic
- Lower Jurassic
- Middle and Upper Triassic

Principal localities throughout the world at which significant fossils of dinosaurs have been found.

I A

AUSTRALIA

world, but also the climates of the lands as well, with the concomitant distributions of plant life. For the world of the Mesozoic was one world climatically just as much as it was one world geographically. It was largely a tropical, subtropical, and warm temperate world.

During the extent of Mesozoic time there was a general uniformity of climates that may be sometimes difficult for us to comprehend, because climatologically speaking we live in an atypical period of earth history. Polar icecaps and strongly banded climatic zones from the equator to the poles seem the natural thing to us, so we are apt to think in such terms when projecting ourselves back through time into the years of the dinosaurs, but when the dinosaurs ruled there were no polar icecaps, while tropical, subtropical, and warm temperate climate extended across the lands of the earth.

Of course the continents were more compactly arranged than they are today, and although the northern and southern limits of Pangaea reached into high latitudes there evidently were no tundra or icefields covering the land. Climates even at such northerly and southerly locations probably were benign.

The general uniformity of Mesozoic climates was associated with a uniformity of topography. Lands generally were low with no great elevations above sea level. There were hills but probably no great mountain ranges to act as barriers to the circulation of moisture-laden winds or to the movements of large, active animals. (The uplifting of our modern mountain systems was to begin during the final stages of Cretaceous history and to extend into the early and middle stages of the Cenozoic Era, after the dinosaurs had become extinct.) This is not to say that any particular dinosaur individuals wandered widely, although it is possible that some of them did migrate over considerable distances, but rather that they extended their ranges of distribution, mile after mile and year after year, until single or closely related species of dinosaurs occupied large territories on the ancient continents. Since there were no insurmountable mountain ranges and extreme climatic barriers to prevent their spreading far and wide, identical or closely related dinosaurs frequently became established throughout the length and breadth of Pangaea during late Triassic, Jurassic, and Cretaceous time, as we have seen.

Megazostrodon, from the Upper Triassic beds of South Africa, was one of the earliest mammals and was closely related to mammals found in Wales and Arizona. It was very small and lived in a microenvironment removed from and beneath the larger world of the dinosaurs. Here *Megazostrodon*, a precursor of the animals that millions of years later were to dominate the earth, confronts a cockroach, whose ancestors predated the little mammal by more than one hundred million years and whose descendants are still very much with us.

Yet there were water barriers that limited the distributions of some dinosaurs, especially during late Cretaceous time. At that stage of earth history there was a long, north-to-south shallow seaway occupying the central part of the North American continent, and likewise a similar seaway, the Turgai Strait, as it has been called, running through Asia to separate what is now Europe from what is now central and eastern Asia. It would appear that these two water barriers confined certain dinosaurs, notably the ceratopsians, to the western part of present North America and the eastern part of present Asia. In the large view, however, most of the dinosaurs enjoyed the freedom to extend their territories to great limits.

So far our attention has been directed at the dinosaurs in their Mesozoic world, because the dinosaurs are our central concern. It must be remembered, however, that the dinosaurs were not alone in their habitats. Although usually dominant, they shared their environments with other animals, some of which had decided impacts on the lives of the dinosaurs, others of which the dinosaurs probably largely ignored.

Many of the first dinosaurs, of late Triassic age, were small and far from being dominant in their surroundings. *Coelophysis*, for example, ran lightly across the late Triassic landscape of present-day New Mexico, but this little dinosaur certainly would have been wary of the large phytosaurs, the crocodile-like thecodonts that lived in the rivers and swamps of those days. The phytosaurs were truly dominant then and there; the small dinosaurs played a secondary role within the association of late Triassic animals. The same probably was true to a lesser extent for the late Triassic prosauropod dinosaurs, reptiles that reached lengths of twenty feet or more. Adults very likely were largely immune from attacks by phytosaurs, but the young prosauropods, even up to the stage of adolescent individuals, must have been vulnerable.

This brings up another consideration, namely that very young dinosaurs of all kinds were objects of attention from all sorts of predators. The predators were often other dinosaurs—even members of their own species—or other reptiles such as phyto-

The late Cretaceous hadrosaur *Hypacrosaurus* browsing in a forest of broad-leaved trees. For herbivores such as this the early Cretaceous botanical revolution that established various angiosperms, or flowering plants, throughout the world provided a new, luxuriant food supply.

Life was not safe even for some of the larger dinosaurs. Here a young individual of the late Cretaceous horned dinosaur *Chasmosaurus* is attacked by a gigantic fifty-foot-long crocodile, *Phobosuchus*.

saurs in the Triassic, and crocodiles, which supplanted the phytosaurs in the Jurassic and Cretaceous. Large lizards may have preyed upon baby dinosaurs in Jurassic and Cretaceous settings, while in Cretaceous time perhaps some of the flying reptiles, some of the early birds, and even the early mammals probably fed upon newly hatched dinosaurs.

Even the large dinosaurs were subject to predation, in many instances of course from giant carnivorous dinosaurs. But in late Cretaceous times there were some gigantic crocodiles, typified by *Phobosuchus* with a length of perhaps forty feet, that could very well have pulled down dinosaurs of considerable size.

Yet the animals that made their livings in part on dinosaurian victims were not necessarily all large.

Some of the small carnivorous dinosaurs as well as lizards and primitive birds undoubtedly robbed dinosaur nests, just as today the African monitor lizard preys upon the nests of crocodiles.

As opposed to such attacks on the dinosaurs, old and young, and on their eggs, many Mesozoic animals were likely ignored by the dinosaurs; they were too insignificant for attention. Such were the small reptiles and amphibians and such were the Mesozoic mammals, uniformly small and retiring during the long years that dinosaurs dominated the earth. These Mesozoic mammals probably were numerous, as are rodents today, but they lived in the undergrowth of ancient forests, hiding from reptilian predators of all kinds.

Lesser predators as well as other kinds of reptiles would have given way to a gigantic sauropod or a ceratopsian walking across the land, just as today almost all animals on the African veldt give way to an elephant or a troupe of elephants, or to a rhinoceros. Such animals are immune from attack and they know it.

In the world of dinosaurs there were the scavengers, as there are today. We can suppose that many of the carnivorous dinosaurs were part-time scavengers, paralleling in this respect various carnivorous mammals. It is much less work for a carnivore to feed upon a carcass than to have to kill its prey, and since most carnivores are and have been opportunists there is reason to think that the predatory dinosaurs derived part of their diet from already dead animals.

It would appear that perhaps some of the pterosaurs, or flying reptiles, also were scavengers. In recent years the bones of a gigantic pterosaur with a wing span of more than forty feet have been discovered in the Upper Cretaceous dinosaur-bearing beds of Texas. This pterosaur had not only an enormous wing span but also a long neck. The suggestion has been made that it may have been a reptilian version, on a giant scale, of a modern vulture, that perhaps it soared in the skies on its great wings to drop down and feed upon the carcasses of giant dinosaurs. The long neck would have enabled it to reach into the interior of huge carcasses.

From what has been described we may envision the world in which the dinosaurs lived as a vast, connected, continental world, stretching around half the circumference of the globe and almost from one pole to its antipodean counterpart, and clothed over much of its surface with extensive forests and savannahs. In the beginning the forests were of primitive aspect, being composed of conifers and cycads and tree ferns, with understories of ground ferns and other simple plants. There were no grasses to form a ground cover, and there were few colorful flowers to add variety to the scene. In the end the forests were of modern aspect, dominated by deciduous trees of familiar appearance—oaks, willows, sassafras, magnolias, poplars, and the like—and livened by a host of flowering plants that lent variety to the landscape. The dinosaurs of late Cretaceous time lived in woodlands that would seem very familiar to our eyes.

It is the nature of the Mesozoic plant associations that afford such important clues as to Mesozoic climates. The plants were primarily of types that grew in gentle climates, where there were rains but no snows, where there were winds but no icy blizzards. They were plants of the sort that one finds today in the Amazonian jungles, in the woodlands of Central America, or in the Florida peninsula. In such environments the dinosaurs prospered. This was the world in which the dinosaurs lived, a great continental world of low lands and small hills, of mild climates, and of luxuriant forests where the living was easy.

EXTINCTION

An egg of the Upper Cretaceous sauropod *Hypselosaurus* from southern France compared with a hen's egg. Many eggs of *Hypselosaurus* seem to have very thin shells. It has been suggested that such eggs were not viable, being similar in this respect to the thin-shelled and nonviable eggs of modern ospreys, caused by excessive amounts of DDT in the diet. Might a causative factor similar to this have brought about the extinction of the dinosaurs?

Whenever and wherever the discussion is concerned with dinosaurs the inevitable question arises: why did they become extinct? It is a good question for which there is no satisfactory answer. Before exploring it, let us look at the facts of the extinction of the dinosaurs.

As we have seen, the dinosaurs of late Cretaceous age lived throughout the world in numbers and variety that had never been approached by their predecessors. They dominated the continents as the continents never before had been dominated, and it would seem that they were so securely established on the earth as to continue for ages into the indefinite future. Then they became extinct, with a geological abruptness that cannot be doubted. It is all in the fossil record.

Thus in many parts of the world the bones of dinosaurs are found in sediments of latest Cretaceous age, while in the earliest post-Cretaceous sediments, of Paleocene age, no dinosaur bones are to be found. To be sure, there have been instances

nation. Recent studies in field and laboratory of the American alligator have shown that sex in these reptiles is determined by temperatures at which the eggs are incubated. If the temperature in the nest is below eighty-six degrees Fahrenheit females are hatched; if above ninety-three degrees Fahrenheit males are produced. Similar studies of incubating turtles have shown analagous results.

Might temperatures of incubating eggs have caused the extinction of the dinosaurs? If there was a sudden change in temperature at the end of Cretaceous time, either up or down, might not this have resulted in the production of only one sex among the dinosaurs, with consequent extinction?

In answer to this the larger problem of other reptiles again may be raised. If there was such a change in temperature it certainly did not affect the crocodiles (close relatives of the dinosaurs) or the turtles. Furthermore there is the problem of parthenogenesis, or asexual reproduction, among reptiles. Studies of lizards have shown that in certain groups females produce females, generation after generation, without the intervention of males. How can we be certain that the absence of one sex through several generations was necessarily fatal to the continuation of the dinosaurs?

It is unlikely that dinosaurs died out because of the "greenhouse effect." We know that there was a retreat at the end of Cretaceous time of shallow seas that had invaded many continental areas during the late stages of Mesozoic history. It has been argued that because of this there was a marked reduction of marine plants, with a consequent increase of carbon dioxide in the atmosphere. An increase in atmospheric carbon dioxide would have resulted in a "greenhouse effect" whereby heat from the surface of the earth could not escape into space. A variation of this theory has to do with the formation of the immense Deccan volcanic flow that covers an area of more than a hundred thousand square miles in India. It has been suggested that the eruption causing the accumulation of such a large body of volcanic rock saturated the atmosphere with carbon dioxide, thus leading to a greenhouse effect. This in turn would have caused a global temperature rise, which in turn would have caused the death of the dinosaurs. Once again, one may ask, "why only the dinosaurs?" Why were other animals, especially many

---

At the very close of the reign of dinosaurs, as recorded in the Upper Edmonton Formation of Alberta, the Hell Creek Formation of Montana, and the Lance Formation of Wyoming, it would appear that the horned dinosaur *Triceratops* was remarkably abundant in what is now western North America. Among the dinosaur assemblages found in the formations named above, the remains of *Triceratops* range from about thirty percent to almost seventy-five percent of the totals. The duck-billed dinosaur *Anatosaurus* may represent as much as twenty-five percent of the total in some regions, but generally less. Other dinosaurs are in lesser numbers, these being armored dinosaurs, some small ornithopods, rare representation of sauropods, and of course the carnivores. This is not a varied list as compared with the wealth of dinosaur types found in Upper Cretaceous beds of an earlier age. It would seem that perhaps the dinosaurs were on a decline during the final years of Cretaceous history, but a decline marked by large numbers of *Triceratops*. One gets an impression that the twilight of the dinosaurs was the time when *Triceratops* wandered across the western lands in great herds, anticipating by millions of years the time when this region would be the home of immense herds of bison. The herds of *Triceratops* suddenly disappeared, or so it seems to us—looking at the event from a vantage point sixty-five million years afterward, and the herds of bison almost disappeared. We know what caused the near-extinction of the bison; we probably shall never know what caused the complete disappearance of *Triceratops*.

---

heat-sensitive reptiles, exempt? (As a sidelight, it should be pointed out that numerous scientists are today worried about a possible greenhouse effect resulting from our consumption of fossil fuels, with the resulting release of carbon dioxide into the air. If such should eventuate during the next century or two or three, there would be the possibility of a melting of the Antarctic ice cap. This in turn would raise sea levels all over the world on the order of about two hundred feet, thereby flooding coastal cities and vast tracts of low farmlands. It is something to think about.)

It is unlikely that dinosaurs became extinct

because they were too big. This idea has already been discussed. Gigantic dinosaurs were successful for millions of years, as were small dinosaurs. Something other than size must have been involved.

It is unlikely that dinosaurs became extinct because of disease and epidemics. This is a difficult explanation to accept. Diseases and epidemics are generally rather specific in their effects; closely related animals may suffer from the same diseases, but more distantly related forms are usually immune. There were many genera and species of dinosaurs, belonging to numerous families and higher categories, these in turn belonging to two quite distinct reptilian orders. It is difficult to imagine any disease or series of diseases that would almost simultaneously affect such a wide spectrum of reptiles.

It is unlikely that dinosaurs became extinct because of starvation. This seems like a fantastic idea. There is a suggestion that the herbivorous dinosaurs starved because they were unable to become adapted to the changes in plant life that took place during Cretaceous time, and with their disappearance there was the correlative disappearance of the carnivorous dinosaurs that fed upon them. But the great plant revolution took place during early Cretaceous time, and the result of this profound change in plant life—the development of the angiosperms, or flowering plants—had just the opposite effect. The appearance of an abundant new food supply was accompanied by an increase of the herbivorous dinosaurs both in numbers and variety, much to the benefit, of course, of the meat-eating dinosaurs. Furthermore, what about the small carnivorous dinosaurs that probably fed upon lizards and other small game? It would seem logical to suppose that they were outside prey-predator relationship of the giants, and therefore should not have been affected.

A variant and perhaps a somewhat more realistic version of this theme is that the plants on which the herbivores fed were lacking in certain elements, such as calcium, that were crucial to their survival. But this does not seem likely, and moreover, as in the related theory, one has to account for the small meat-eating dinosaurs.

It is unlikely that dinosaurs were poisoned. Another fantastic theory, it would seem. Modern experiments seem to show that turtles, for example, are not particularly sensitive to the taste of plants. Therefore, it is argued, there may have been poisons in some of the Cretaceous plants that brought about the end of the herbivorous dinosaurs, and correlatively of the carnivores. It must be realized, however, that the turtles were around in great numbers during Cretaceous time, and the insensitive turtles, presumably prone to eat anything that came their way, lived through the Cretaceous-Cenozoic transition with the greatest of success.

It is unlikely that dinosaurs became extinct as a result of egg predation. A very old theory is that the dinosaurs were wiped out because early mammals of Cretaceous time robbed their nests. It is likely that many dinosaur nests were destroyed by primitive mammals, and by lizards and various small dinosaurs, searching for eggs to eat. Yet it is doubtful that such depredations in themselves could have brought about the end of the dinosaurs. Modern crocodiles are subject to egg predation from lizards, while sea turtles similarly suffer from various mammals, but unless such predation is aided and abetted by human hunters there are enough hatchlings in the long run to perpetuate the species. These reptiles have a shotgun approach to re-

production; if there are enough eggs some will hatch and some of the young reptiles will survive all the hazards surrounding them, to grow into adults.

It is unlikely that dinosaurs became extinct because their eggs ceased to be viable. It has been noted that the shells of the dinosaur eggs found in southern France, the eggs attributed to the Upper Cretaceous sauropod dinosaur *Hypselosaurus*, seem to be unusually thin. From this observation a theory has been advanced that such eggs eventually ceased to be viable, so that the dinosaurs failed to reproduce. A parallel is drawn with the eggs of some raptorial birds, such as ospreys, among which the shells have become fragile, affected by DDT in the diets of the parent birds, resulting in failures to reproduce. A deterioration of the eggs in *Hypselosaurus* is an interesting but a very tentative idea; whether it can be applied to the many species of dinosaurs is questionable.

It is unlikely that dinosaurs died out because of racial senescence. This is one of the early theories. There was the hypothesis that species, like individuals, went through a sort of life cycle—of birth, adolescence, maturity, old age, and death—and according to this idea the time had come for the dinosaurs to die. Such a theory is more in the realm of philosophy than of science; there is no evidence to support it.

It is unlikely that dinosaurs became extinct because of ecological replacement. During Cretaceous time the early mammals were evolving in numbers and variety. And although these very primitive mammals were small and seemingly insignificant, it has been argued that they may have eaten the food out from under the noses of the herbivorous dinosaurs. Perhaps, if they could not destroy the dinosaurs by eating their eggs, they could do so by eating their food supply. This is a possibility, but it does not seem very probable. It would require virtual plagues of small mammals to have reduced the natural forage to such a degree as to starve out the herbivorous dinosaurs. There certainly is nothing in the paleontological evidence to support this idea. The Mesozoic mammals would seem to have been held in check as long as dinosaurs were on the earth. It was only after the extinction of the dinosaurs that the early mammals truly expanded to occupy the lands. In other words, the disappearance of the dinosaurs created vacancies within many ecological niches that were then quickly filled by mammals descended from ancestors that had been contemporaneous with the dinosaurs. As a sidelight it should be mentioned that in our modern world any plague of small mammals, notably rodents, is usually quickly self-destructive. The population of lemmings, for example, will rise to such heights that these little rodents cover the land. Then they quickly disappear; many of them rush frantically across the land to plunge into the sea.

It is unlikely that dinosaurs became extinct because of reversals in the earth's magnetic field. Recent research has shown that the magnetic field of the earth is reversed at intervals through time. Moreover it has been noted that there would seem to have been extinction of microscopic marine organisms at the time of some magnetic reversals, for what reason it is hard to say. Would any magnetic reversal have affected the dinosaurs, and if so, why? If so, why not other reptiles, notably those ubiquitous crocodiles? It is all a matter for speculation.

It is unlikely that dinosaurs became extinct because of extraterrestrial events. The theories for the extinction of the dinosaurs so far enumerated (and they by no means exhaust the possibilities) are theories having to do with terrestrial events. There is another category of theories, and these are the ones that rely upon extraterrestrial or cosmic events to account for the disappearance of the dinosaurs. Three such theories will be discussed, namely that the dinosaurs were destroyed by the explosion of a supernova in space, that they were destroyed by a comet striking the earth, and that they were destroyed by the collision of the earth with a huge meteor or asteroid.

It is unlikely that dinosaurs became extinct because of a supernova explosion. The first of the extraterrestrial theories supposes that there was an explosion of a supernova in "nearby" space, such an explosion releasing enormous amounts of energy that would have affected the earth. The results of the explosion might have been in the first place the bombardment of the earth with great amounts of cosmic and gamma rays during the early phases of the outburst, these having adverse effects upon the life of the earth. Secondly, such an event might have affected the climate in such a way as to bring about the extinction of many forms of life. The supernova theory has the merit of explaining the sudden and wide-spread extinctions that characterized the end of Cretaceous time, but there still remains the old stumbling block of selectivity. How could such an event have brought about the extinction of the dinosaurs, and the marine reptiles of late Cretaceous age, and spared so many other inhabitants of the globe? This is still the unanswered question.

It is unlikely that dinosaurs became extinct because a comet collided with the earth. The comet theory supposes that when a heavenly body of this type struck the earth there was a tremendous amount of atmospheric heating that would have killed off the dinosaurs. At the same time it is supposed that the microscopic marine organisms which would seem to have suffered wide extinction at the end of the Cretaceous Period were killed as a result of cyanide released into the atmosphere by the comet. While this theory explains the demise of the dinosaurs and the marine plankton, it fails to explain how in the face of such an event so many animals managed to survive. Could so great a catastrophe have been so selective?

It is unlikely that dinosaurs became extinct because an asteroid collided with the earth. The newest and perhaps the most elaborate extraterrestrial theory invokes the collision of the earth with a giant meteorite or asteroid, as much as six to twelve miles in diameter. The basis for this idea has been the recent discovery of a clay layer of very late Cretaceous age containing abnormal amounts of the element iridium, as much as twenty times the amount as is usually found in rocks. Iridium is a common element in meteorites, although it is a rare earth element. It is suggested that upon impact of a meteorite with the earth such a great amount of dust particles would have been thrown up into the atmosphere as to obliterate the sunlight for three or four years, thereby killing much of the earth's plant life, which depends upon photosynthesis to survive. Of course the disappearance of plants would have brought about the disappearance of the plant-eating dinosaurs, and in turn the carnivorous dinosaurs that depended upon the giant herbivores. But once again we run into the problem of selectivity. Furthermore it can be doubted that a collision taking place at one particular spot on the surface of the

Upper Z Coal→

Lower Z Coal→

Disappearance of dinosaurs

Paleocene

Cretaceous

Tullock Formation

Hell Creek Formation

In Montana the uppermost Cretaceous sediments are represented by the Hell Creek Formation, which is succeeded by the Paleocene Tullock Formation. There are two coal seams in the Tullock Formation known as the "upper Z coal" (rather thick) and the "lower Z coal" (quite thin). The lower Z coal is regarded as constituting the base of the Tullock Formation. But as is apparent in the photograph, taken in northeastern Montana, there is no real break in sedimentation.

David Archibald of Yale University and William Clemens of the University of California at Berkeley have carried on extensive field studies of the Hell Creek–Tullock sequence at more than two hundred sites, and have found that dinosaurs characteristic of the Hell Creek beds disappear about nine feet below the lower Z coal. Associated with these last dinosaurs are characteristic Cretaceous mammals.

At certain sites in Montana studied by Robert Sloan of the University of Minnesota and Leigh van Valen of Chicago University, there are found within the upper eighty feet of the Hell Creek Formation primitive Paleocene-type mammals associated with Cretaceous mammals and dinosaurs. As one proceeds upward through this sequence the species of Paleocene-type mammals increase from five to thirteen while the species of typical Cretaceous mammals decrease from nineteen to two. The dinosaurs likewise show a marked decrease (a tenfold decline in *Triceratops* for example), eventually to disappear.

Here in Montana we see the extinction of the dinosaurs, the end of Cretaceous history, and the advent of Paleocene history, all contained within a few feet of conformable sediments. Here there is no evidence for a big-bang extinction of the dinosaurs.

globe, no matter how massive, would have caused world-wide effects.

A recent weakening of the asteroid collision theory has resulted from the discovery at Hell Creek, Montana (mentioned above), of the transition from dinosaur-bearing to early mammal-bearing sediments, all within a very short vertical distance, and lying well *below* the iridium layer. This would seem to show that the extinction took place in a nonviolent fashion, and that the accumulation of the iri-

dium layer, whatever its effects might have been, occurred at a time significantly after the disappearance of the dinosaurs.

Serious doubts as to the reality of the asteroid hypothesis also have been raised by the occurrences of fossil plants. This evidence is of paramount importance, because plants form the base of the food chain on the earth, and serious disruptions of plant life on the earth caused by an earth-encircling cloud of dust that effectively blocked the sun and drastically reduced photosynthesis would have had cumulative effects on the land animals probably beyond anything seen in the fossil record.

One problem is that although there were considerable extinctions of plants during the Cretaceous-Cenozoic transition, these were not synchronous with the extinctions of the dinosaurs; rather they came *after* the dinosaurs had disappeared. Furthermore the extinctions of plants were geographically diverse and generally moderate. For example, one would expect that the northernmost plants of the time, adapted to dormancy during winter seasons, would have survived a prolonged period of adverse conditions caused by a dust cloud blocking much of the sunlight reaching the earth, while the tropical plants, having no such mechanisms for survival, would have suffered widespread extinction. Just the opposite happened; the greatest loss of plant life after the Cretaceous was among some of the northern flowering plants. This reduction of plants took place during early Paleocene time, within the first epoch of the Cenozoic Era, when the dinosaurs were long gone and mammals were inheriting the lands.

The reduction of plants at this time did not last long; by late Paleocene time there was a strong recovery, and plants continued to prosper during the Age of Mammals. It would seem probable that this temporary setback among some floras of the world—at worst of moderate dimensions and seemingly irregularly effective across the continents—was the result of a short-lived lowering of temperatures following the Cretaceous-Paleocene transition.

Such moderate and diverse extinctions among the plants of the world, occurring not at the time of dinosaurian extinction, but afterward, do not accord with a sudden catastrophic event taking place at the end of Cretaceous time. In summary, the meteorite collision hypothesis leaves much to be desired. It is too soon at this date to draw any hard conclusions as to the significance of the iridium layer, where it is found.

After all of the hauling and backing, after looking at the many theories that have been advanced to account for the disappearance of the dinosaurs, we have made a full circle and are back at the starting point. No one theory and not even a combination of theories can satisfactorily account for the extinction of the dinosaurs, but not the extinction of crocodiles and other reptiles, for the extinction of the late Cretaceous marine reptiles and much planktonic life, but not the extinction of the ever-burgeoning bony fishes in the seas. The big-bang ideas of extraterrestrial catastrophies have too many loopholes to provide satisfactory explanations for the disappearance of the dinosaurs. The less spectacular earthbound theories likewise fail to explain the phenomenon in all of its aspects.

In short, the extinction of the dinosaurs is a constantly baffling problem, as much of a mystery now as it was a half century or a century ago. We probably shall never know why these fabulous reptiles, so long the masters of the continents, should have disappeared completely from the earth. It seems likely that this will remain in the future, as it has in the past, one of the unanswered problems of paleontology.

Overleaf: Did the explosion of a supernova sixty-five million years ago, with consequent high energy radiation, cause the extinction of the dinosaurs? If so, why did so many other forms of life survive the crisis? In this scene a waning supernova shines on a dead *Ankylosaurus*.

WHERE TO SEE DINOSAURS

Opportunities to see dinosaur skeletons, or even a single skeleton, are at best limited. It is one thing to go into the field and find dinosaur bones; it is something else to locate a dinosaur skeleton, dig it out of the ground in the proper way, transport it to a laboratory, clean and prepare the fossil bones so that they will be immune to the ravages of time, humidity, or dessication, and finally to assemble them as an articulated skeleton in a museum hall. Such procedures are time-consuming and expensive, especially in terms of man-hours, man-months, and man-years. Consequently many institutions, be they museums or universities, shy away from programs of dinosaur research.

The greatest number of dinosaur exhibits is to be found in North America. The more important displays may be listed as follows.

Several museums have extensive exhibits of mounted skeletons, notably the American Museum of Natural History in New York (perhaps the most numerous collection of skeletons to be seen in the world), the Smithsonian Institution in Washington, the Royal Ontario Museum in Toronto, the National Museum of Canada in Ottawa, the Peabody Museum at Yale University, the Carnegie Museum in Pittsburgh, the Field Museum in Chicago, and the Los Angeles County Museum.

In other institutions there are lesser displays of dinosaur skeletons, in some cases a single skeleton. These are the Museum of Comparative Zoology at Harvard University, the Academy of Natural Science in Philadelphia, the geology museum at Princeton University, the Cleveland Museum of Natural History, museums at the University of Michigan, the University of Nebraska, the University of Wisconsin, the University of Kansas, the University of Oklahoma, the Texas Memorial Museum at the University of Texas, the University of Utah, Brigham Young University in Provo, the Utah Field House in Vernal, the geology museum at the University of Wyoming, the Denver Museum, the California Academy of Science in San Francisco, the geology museum at the University of California at Berkeley, the Carter County Museum in Ekalaka, Montana; and, in Alberta, Canada, the University of Alberta in Edmonton, and the Tyrrell Museum of Paleontology in Drumheller.

One of the most unusual displays of dinosaurs is the massive accumulation of bones in the rock, as seen at Dinosaur National Monument in Utah. Likewise dinosaur skeletons in place are to be seen at Dinosaur Provincial Park in Alberta. There should also be mentioned the *in situ* displays of dinosaur footprints, to be seen at various localities in North America, and on other continents as well. Perhaps the finest such example of dinosaur footprints in place is at Rocky Hill, Connecticut, where hundreds of tracks of Triassic dinosaurs are exposed. A fine collection of Triassic tracks is at the museum of Amherst College. Trackways of giant Cretaceous dinosaurs are to be seen near Glen Rose, Texas.

In South America there are displays of dinosaur skeletons at the Argentine Museum of Natural Science in Buenos Aires and at the Museum of La Plata, Argentina.

In Europe dinosaur displays are to be seen at the British Museum (Natural History) in London, the Belgian Royal Museum of Natural History in Brussels (where the series of *Iguanodon* skeletons probably constitutes the largest exhibit of a single species of dinosaur), the National Museum of Natural History in Paris, the Senckenberg Museum in Frankfurt, the University of Tübingen in Germany, the University of Zürich, Switzerland, the University of Uppsala, Sweden, and the Paleontological Institute of the Academy of Science of the USSR in Moscow. Extensive collections of Mongolian dinosaurs have been made by the Polish Academy of Science in Warsaw, but at the present time these are not on exhibit.

In Asia there is a sauropod skeleton at the Indian Statistical Institute in Calcutta, the only mounted dinosaur skeleton in India. Other dinosaur skeletons are at the National Science Museum in Tokyo and the natural his-

tory museum in Osaka. Excellent skeletons collected in China are at the Institute of Vertebrate Paleontology in Peking. Mongolian dinosaurs are at the museum in Ulan Bator.

In Africa there are dinosaurs at the South African Museum in Capetown, and at the Bernhard Price Institute of Palaeontology at Witwatersrand University, Johannesburg.

Dinosaur materials are in the Queensland Museum in Brisbane, Australia.

This brief review of where to see dinosaurs is certainly incomplete; apologies are extended to any institutions inadvertently omitted from this listing. New discoveries of dinosaurs are constantly being made, and frequently such finds are placed on exhibition. Thus it is difficult to keep any list such as this completely up to date.

BIBLIOGRAPHY

There is a vast body of literature on dinosaurs, most of it highly technical. The following list is restricted to a few general books and articles on the subject, many of which are presently available.

de Camp, Sprague, and Catherine de Camp. *The Day of the Dinosaur*. New York: Doubleday, 1968.

Charig, Alan. *A New Look at the Dinosaurs*. New York: Mayflower Books, 1979.

Charig, Alan, and Brenda Horsfield. *Before the Ark*. London: British Broadcasting Corporation, 1975.

Colbert, Edwin H. *Dinosaurs: Their Discovery and Their World*. New York: E. P. Dutton, 1961.

———. *The Age of Reptiles*. New York: W. W. Norton, 1965.

———. *Men and Dinosaurs: The Search in Field and Laboratory*. New York: E. P. Dutton, 1968.

———. *The Dinosaur World*. (Illustrated by George Geygan and Paul Geygan.) New York: Stravon Educational Press, 1977.

———. *The Year of the Dinosaur*. (Illustrated by Margaret Colbert.) New York: Scribner's, 1977.

Cox, Barry. *Prehistoric Animals*. New York: Grosset and Dunlap, 1970.

Desmond, Adrian J. *The Hot-Blooded Dinosaurs*. New York: Dial Press/James Wade, 1976.

Glut, Donald F. *The New Dinosaur Dictionary*. (With Introductions by Ralph E. Molnar and Robert A. Long.) Secaucus, New Jersey: Citadel Press, 1982.

Halstead, L. B., and Jenny Halstead. *Dinosaurs*. Poole, Dorset: Blandford Press, 1981.

Hotton, Nicholas III. *Dinosaurs*. New York: Pyramid Publications, 1963.

Kurtén, Björn. *The Age of Dinosaurs*. New York: McGraw-Hill, 1968.

Life before Man. New York: Time-Life Books, 1972.

Ostrom, John H. "A New Look at Dinosaurs." (Paintings by Roy Andersen.) *National Geographic*, Vol. 154, No. 2 (1978): 152–185.

———. *Dinosaurs*. Burlington, North Carolina: Carolina Biological Supply Company, 1981.

Russell, Dale A. *A Vanished World: The Dinosaurs of Western Canada*. (Photographs by Susanne M. Swibold. Paintings by Eleanor M. Kish.) Ottawa: National Museums of Canada, 1977.

Špinar, Zdeněk V. *Life before Man*. (Illustrated by Zdeněk Burian.) London: Thames and Hudson, 1972.

Stout, William. *The Dinosaurs: A Fantastic View of a Lost Era*. (Illustrated by William Stout, narrated by William Service, edited by Byron Preiss.) New York: Bantam Books, 1981.

Swinton, W. E. *The Dinosaurs*. New York: Wiley, 1970.

———. *The Wonderful World of Prehistoric Animals*. (Paintings by Maurice Wilson.) Garden City, New York: Garden City Books, 1971.

Thomas, Roger D. K., and Everett C. Olson, eds. *A Cold Look at the Warm-Blooded Dinosaurs*. American Association for the Advancement of Science Symposia Series, No. 28. Boulder, Colorado: Westview Press, 1980.

White, Theodore E. *Dinosaurs—at Home*. New York: Vantage Press, 1967.

GLOSSARY

The names of dinosaurs are difficult for many people, and so they ask why these ancient reptiles should have such unfamiliar and seemingly tongue-twisting names. The answer to this question is that there are no common names for the dinosaurs; they go by their scientific names.

Scientific nomenclature for plants and animals was devised by the great Swedish botanist Carl von Linné, more familiarly known as Linnaeus, in the middle of the eighteenth century. The modern nomenclature of plants and animals is based upon the tenth edition of his *System Naturae,* published in 1758. According to the Linnaean system, known as binomial nomenclature, every distinct animal and plant, living and fossil, has two names, a generic name that establishes the general relationships of the organism, and a specific or trivial name that places the organism in its own category, apart from anything else. The generic name comes first and its initial letter is capitalized; the specific name follows without any capitals.

Scientifically the horse is *Equus caballus* in all languages of the world, and thus is immediately recognized for what it is: the genus *Equus*, the species *caballus*. But there are other species of *Equus*, such as the ass *Equus asinus*, and the various zebras. So these animals are grouped in higher categories according to their relationships; the asses, horses, and zebras belonging to the family Equidae. The Equidae in turn belong within a still higher category, the odd-toed hoofed mammals of the order Perissodactyla, a group that includes also the rhi-noceroses and tapirs. The perissodactyls in turn belong to the great class of Mammalia, one of several classes making up the backboned animals, or Chordata. The chordates comprise one phylum of the animal kingdom. Plants are likewise classified and categorized. Thus there is an international language for the designation of living and extinct organisms. Many living animals and plants have common names in the multitudinous languages of the world, but for fossils there are no such common names.

The scientific name of an organism is established by the first person to describe the plant or animal in a reputable scientific publication. This person has the honor and responsibility of choosing the name.

Scientific names are generally based upon the classical tongues, Greek and Latin. The names commonly have Greek roots that are latinized. However, names may be based on any of the modern languages and may combine modern and classical roots in a single name. Some names are even made up by arbitrary combinations of letters.

Names are frequently chosen to try to express some character or attribute of the plant or animal in question. Once published a name cannot be changed, even though it may turn out to be inappropriate. For example the Triassic reptile *Phytosaurus* was first described by Georg Friedrich von Jaeger in 1828 on the basis of very incomplete fossil material. He thought this was a plant-eating reptile (*phyton*, a plant; *sauros*, reptile). Good fossils show quite clearly that *Phytosaurus* was carnivorous, but the name stands.

It must be remembered that these names are designations and not descriptions, and they should be treated as such. Therefore one should not worry about the appropriateness of the name. Today we do not expect everybody named Taylor to make clothes or everybody named Miller to grind flour.

Species do not figure in this book; they are appropriate for more detailed discussions than are to be found in these pages. Therefore the genus is the basic category for the descriptions and discussions appearing here.

A word about *saurus*. The Greek *sauros* originally meant a lizard, but it has come to represent in the minds of zoologists and paleontologists the more general category of reptiles. It is here used in the latter sense.

The pronunciation of scientific names is not difficult if one takes the time to analyze the components of the name. Knowledge of Greek and Latin is very helpful, but today most people have not studied these languages. (Interestingly, although many adults struggle with the names of dinosaurs children master the designations with little difficulty.) Pronunciation is something of a personal matter. Names derived from Greek and Latin words are usually accented on the next to last syllable, sometimes on the preceding or antepenultimate syllable. There is no C in the Greek alphabet. The Greek K is often transliterated into C. American usage generally gives such a C a soft or S sound; British usage generally retains the hard or K sound.

The symbols that are used to indicate the pronunciation of the terms listed are largely self-explanatory, but a brief key may be found below. It should be noted that our spoken language contains a great many unstressed syllables in which the vowel, although sounded, is obscure, like the *a* in *alone* or the *u* in *circus*. In the pronunciation guide, these vowels are printed in italics.

Pronunciation Key

Consonants represent their customary sounds. The combination "th" is sounded as in *thin*.
Vowel sounds are as follows:

a	at	e	met	ī	bite	oo	soon
a	alone	*e*	system	o	not	u	up
ä	are	ē	meet	*o*	vigor	*u*	circus
ā	date	i	bit	ō	note	ū	unit
aw	saw	*i*	easily	oi	oil		

Alamosaurus (al' *a* mō saw' r*u*s; *Alamo* from Ojo Alamo in New Mexico + *sauros* reptile). Perhaps the last of the sauropods, of late Cretaceous age, from New Mexico. Naabashito Member of the Kirtland Formation.

Albertosaurus (al burr' t*o* saw' r*u*s; *Alberta* a Canadian province + *sauros* reptile). A large Upper Cretaceous carnosaur from Alberta. Oldman Formation.

Allosaurus (al *o* saw' r*u*s; *allos* strange + *sauros* reptile). An Upper Jurassic carnosaur from western North America. Morrison Formation.

Altispinax (al t*i* spī' nax; *alti* high + *spina* spine). A Lower Cretaceous carnivorous dinosaur from Europe, in which the spines of the vertebrae are greatly elongated.

Anatosaurus (*a* nat *o* saw' r*u*s; *anatos* harmless + *sauros* reptile). An Upper Cretaceous hadrosaur from western North America. Lance Formation.

Anchiceratops (an' kī ser' *a* tops; *anchion* near + *keratos* horn + *ops* face). An Upper Cretaceous horned dinosaur from Alberta. Edmonton Formation.

Ankylosauria (an' k*i* lō saw' rē *a*; *ankylos* to grow together + *sauros* reptile). The suborder of armored dinosaurs, of Cretaceous age.

Ankylosaurus (an' k*i* lō saw' r*u*s; *ankylos* to grow together + *sauros* reptile). An Upper Cretaceous armored dinosaur from Montana. Hell Creek Formation.

Apatosaurus (*a* pat *o* saw' r*u*s; *apate* deceit, illusory + *sauros* reptile). A very large Upper Jurassic sauropod from western North America. Commonly known as *Brontosaurus*. Morrison Formation.

Archaeopteryx (är' kē op' t*e* rix; *archaeos* primitive + *pteros* wing). The first bird, of late Jurassic age, from the Solnhofen limestone of southern Germany. Solnhofen Formation.

Arrhinoceratops (ā rī' nō ser' *a* tops; *ar* without + *rhinos* nose + *keratos* horn + *ops* face). An Upper Cretaceous horned dinosaur from Alberta. Edmonton Formation.

Aublysodon (ō blis' *o* don). See *Albertosaurus*.

Barapasaurus (b*a* rap *a* saw' r*u*s; *bara* big + *pa* leg + *sauros* reptile). *Barapa* is derived from Indian languages). A Lower Jurassic sauropod from central India; perhaps the oldest of the sauropods. Kota Formation.

Brachiosaurus (brak' ē ō saw' r*u*s; *brachion* arm + *sauros* reptile). An extremely large Upper Jurassic sauropod with long fore limbs, from western North America and Tanzania, Africa. Morrison and Tendaguru Formations.

Brontosaurus (bron t*o* saw' r*u*s; *bronte* thunder + *sauros* reptile). See *Apatosaurus*.

Camarasaurus (kam *a* r*a* saw' r*u*s; *kamara* chamber, vault + *sauros* reptile). An Upper Jurassic sauropod of moderate size from western North America. Morrison Formation.

Camptosaurus (kamp t*o* saw' r*u*s; *kamptos* bent + *sauros* reptile). A primitive Upper Jurassic ornithopod from western North America. Morrison Formation.

Carnosauria (kär n*o* saw' rē *a*; *carnis* flesh + *sauros* reptile). A suborder of the theropod dinosaurs; large carnivores.

Centrosaurus (sen tro saw' rus; *kentron* spike or spur + *sauros* reptile). An Upper Cretaceous ceratopsian from Alberta, considered by some paleontologists to be synonymous with *Monoclonius*, by others to be distinct. Oldman Formation.

Ceratopsia (ser a top' se a; *keratos* horn + *ops* face). The suborder of horned dinosaurs of Cretaceous age.

Ceratosaurus (se rat' ō saw' rus; *keratos* horn + *sauros* reptile). A large Upper Jurassic carnosaur from western North America, distinguished by its nasal horn. Morrison Formation.

Cetiosaurus (sē' tē ō saw' rus; *keteios* large + *sauros* reptile). A Jurassic sauropod dinosaur from England. The first sauropod to be discovered. Oxford clays.

Chasmosaurus (kaz mo saw' rus; *chasma* space + *sauros* reptile). An Upper Cretaceous horned dinosaur from Alberta, with a long frill crenulated along its edges. Oldman Formation.

Coelophysis (sē lo fī' sis; *koilos* hollow + *physa* bag). An Upper Triassic coelurosaur from North America. One of the earliest saurischian dinosaurs. Chinle Formation.

Coelurosauria (se loo ro saw' rē a; *koilos* hollow + *ouro* tail + *sauros* reptile). An infraorder of theropod dinosaurs.

Compsognathus (komp sog na' thus; *kompsos* elegant + *gnathos* jaw). An Upper Jurassic coelurosaur from southern Germany. Solnhofen limestone.

Corythosaurus (ko rith o saw' rus; *korythos* helmet + *sauros* reptile). An Upper Cretaceous crested hadrosaur from Alberta. Oldman Formation.

Deinocheirus (dī' nō kī' rus; *deinos* terrible + *cheiros* hand). A gigantic Cretaceous carnivorous dinosaur from Mongolia, presently known only from its fore limbs. Nemegt Formation.

Deinodon (dīn' o don; *deinos* terrible + *odon* tooth). An Upper Cretaceous carnosaur from Montana and Alberta. Judith River and Oldman formations.

Deinonychus (dī' nō nik' us; *deinos* terrible + *onychos* claw). A Lower Cretaceous carnosaur of moderate size from Montana. Cloverly Formation.

Desmatosuchus (dez ma' tō soo' kus; *desmatos* bond + *souchos* crocodile). An Upper Triassic armored thecodont from southwestern United States. Chinle Formation.

Dicynodontia (dī sī' no don' tē a; *di* two + *kynos* dog + *odon* tooth). A suborder of therapsid or mammal-like reptiles, of Permian and Triassic ages and widely distributed throughout the world.

Dilophosaurus (dī lō' fo saw' rus; *di* two + *lophos* crest + *sauros* reptile). An Upper Triassic or Lower Jurassic carnosaur with two longitudinal crests on the skull. From northern Arizona. Kayenta Formation.

Dinosauria (dī no saw' rē a; *deinos* terrible + *sauros* reptile). A general term that includes those Mesozoic reptiles now classified in two orders, Saurischia and Ornithischia.

Diplodocus (dip' lō dō' kus; *diplos* double + *dokos* beam). A slender, very elongated Upper Jurassic sauropod from western North America. Morrison Formation.

Dromaeosaurus (drō' mē o saw' rus; *dromaios* swift-running + *sauros* reptile). A small Upper Cretaceous theropod from Alberta. Oldman Formation.

Dromiceiomimus (drō' mi kā' ō mī' mus; *Dromiceius* the Australian emu + *mimus* mimic). An "ostrich dinosaur" with very large eyes, perhaps as an adaptation for feeding at night. From the Upper Cretaceous Edmonton Formation of Alberta.

Edaphosaurus (e daf' ō saw' rus; *edaphos* earth + *sauros* reptile). A Lower Permian pelycosaur from Texas, noted for the large sail on the back. Wichita and Clear Fork beds.

Edmontosaurus (ed mon' to saw' rus; from the Edmonton Formation + *sauros* reptile). A hadrosaur from the Upper Cretaceous Edmonton Formation of Alberta.

Gorgosaurus (gawr go saw' rus; *gorgos* fear + *sauros* reptile). A large Upper Cretaceous carnosaur from Alberta. See *Albertosaurus*. Oldman Formation.

Hadrosaurus (had ro saw' rus; *hadros* bulky + *sauros* reptile). An Upper Cretaceous "duck-billed" ornithopod dinosaur. This name was given to the first dinosaur skeleton found in North America. Hornerstown marls.

Hesperosuchus (hes' per ō soo' kus; *hesperos* western + *souchos* crocodile). A small thecodont from the Upper Triassic Chinle Formation of Arizona.

Heterodontosaurus (het er o don to saw' rus; *heteros* different + *odon* tooth + *sauros* reptile). An early ornithischian dinosaur from South Africa. Red Beds Formation.

Hylaeosaurus (hī lē' o saw' rus; *hylaios* of the forest + *sauros* reptile). A Lower Cretaceous ankylosaur, or armored ornithischian, from southern England. One of the first dinosaurs to be described. Wealden beds.

Hypacrosaurus (hi pak' ro saw' rus; *hypakros* nearly the highest + *sauros* reptile). A crested hadrosaur from the Upper Cretaceous Edmonton Formation of Alberta, and Two Medicine Formation of Montana.

Hypselosaurus (hip sel' o saw' rus; *hypselos* high + *sauros* reptile). An Upper Cretaceous sauropod from southern France. Large fossil eggs are associated with the remains of this dinosaur. Begudian beds.

Hysilophodon (hip si lof' o don; *hypsi* high + *lophos* crest + *odon* tooth). A small Lower Cretaceous ornithopod of relatively primitive form from southern England. Wealden beds.

Iguanodon (i gwä′ n*o* don; *iguana* a large American lizard + *odon* tooth). A large ornithopod dinosaur from the Lower Cretaceous of Europe. First described by Gideon Mantell. Wealden beds.

Kentrosaurus (ken tr*o* saw′ r*u*s; *kentron* spike + *sauros* reptile). An Upper Jurassic stegosaur from Tanzania, characterized by numerous long spikes on the back and tail. Tendaguru beds.

Kritosaurus (kri t*o* saw′ r*u*s; *kritos* chosen + *sauros* reptile). An Upper Cretaceous hadrosaur from the San Juan Basin of New Mexico. Naabashito Member of the Fruitland Formation.

Labyrinthodontia (lab *i* rin′ thō don′ tē *a*; *labyrinthos* labyrinth + *odon* tooth). A major group of early amphibians ranging in age from the Upper Devonian through the Upper Triassic and widely distributed throughout the world.

Lambeosaurus (lam′ bē ō saw′ r*u*s; *Lambe* Lawrence Lambe, Canadian paleontologist + *sauros* reptile). One of the crested hadrosaurs from Alberta. Oldman Formation.

Leptoceratops (lep t*o* ser′ *a* tops; *leptos* small + *keratos* horn + *ops* face). A small ceratopsian from Alberta, of primitive form even though of a late age in ceratopsian history. Edmonton Formation.

Lesothosaurus (le sō′ thō saw′ r*u*s; *Lesotho* a nation formerly called Basutoland, in southern Africa + *sauros* reptile). A primitive ornithischian from the Upper Triassic of Africa; one of the earliest members of the Ornithischia. Red Beds Formation.

Lufengosaurus (loo fen gō saw′ r*u*s; *Lufeng* a Chinese city + *sauros* reptile). An Upper Triassic prosauropod dinosaur from Yunnan Province, closely related to *Plateosaurus).* Lower Lufeng Formation.

Maiasaura (mī *a* saw′ r*a*; *maia* nurse + *sauros* reptile). A very small hadrosaur, probably represented by juveniles, from Montana.) Two Medicine Formation.

Mamenchisaurus (m*a* men k*i* saw′ r*u*s; *Mamenchi* a Szechuan place name + *sauros* reptile). A large Upper Jurassic sauropod with an exceedingly long neck. From Szechuan, China.

Megalosaurus (meg′ *a* lō saw′ r*u*s; *megale* giant + *sauros* reptile). A large carnosaur of Jurassic to Lower Cretaceous age, widely distributed in Europe. Upper Jurassic and Wealden beds.

Megazostrodon (meg *a* zos′ tr*o* don; *megas* large + *zostron* girdle + *odon* tooth). One of the earliest mammals, from the Upper Triassic of southern Africa. Red Beds Formation.

Metoposaurus (m*e* tō p*o* saw′ r*u*s; *metapon* forehead + *sauros* reptile). A very large Upper Triassic labyrintho-

dont amphibian found in North America, Europe, Africa, and India. Chinle Formation in North America.

Monoclonius (mo′ nō klō′ nē *u*s; *monos* single + *klonion* a young twig). An Upper Cretaceous ceratopsian from Alberta. Oldman Formation.

Ornithischia (awr n*i* this′ kē *a*; *ornithos* bird + *ischion* hip). One of the two orders of dinosaurs, characterized by a pelvis in which the pubic bone is rotated back to lie parallel to the ischium.

Ornitholestes (awr nith′ *o* les′ tēz; *ornithos* bird + *lestes* robber). A small Upper Jurassic theropod from western North America. Morrison Formation.

Ornithopoda (awr n*i* thop′ *o* d*a*; *ornithos* bird + *podos* foot). A suborder of ornithischian dinosaurs.

Pachycephalosaurus (pa k*i* sef′ *a* lō saw′ r*u*s; *pachys* thick + *kephale* head + *sauros* reptile). A large Upper Cretaceous ornithopod with a heavy skull. From western North America. Lance Formation.

Pachyrhinosaurus (pa k*i* rī′ nō saw′ r*u*s; *pachys* thick + *rhinos* nose + *sauros* reptile). An Upper Cretaceous ceratopsian in which there is a thick boss instead of a horn on top of the skull. From Alberta. Edmonton Formation.

Parasaurolophus (pa r*a* saw r*o* lō′ f*u*s; *para* beside + *sauros* reptile + *lophos* crest). An Upper Cretaceous hadrosaur with a very long, hollow crest on the skull. From New Mexico. Fruitland Formation.

Pentaceratops (pen t*a* ser′ *a* tops; *pente* five + *keratos* horn + *ops* face). An Upper Cretaceous ceratopsian with an ornate frill. From New Mexico. Fruitland Formation.

Phobosuchus (fō′ bō soo′ k*u*s; *phobos* fear + *souchos* crocodile). A gigantic Upper Cretaceous crocodile from western North America. Judith River Formation.

Phytosaur (fī′ t*o* sawr; *phyton* plant + *sauros* reptile). A thecodont reptile of late Triassic age.

Placerias (pl*a* ser′ ē *a*s; *plakos* wide.) "Generic name . . . given on account of the breadth of body." A large Upper Triassic dicynodont reptile from southwestern United States. Chinle Formation.

Plateosaurus (plat′ ē *o* saw′ r*u*s; *plate* blade of an oar + *sauros* reptile). A large Upper Triassic prosauropod from southern Germany. Keuper beds.

Polacanthus (pō l*a* kan′ th*u*s; *polos* axis + *akanthus* thorn). A Lower Cretaceous ankylosaur from the Isle of Wight, England. Wealden beds.

Procompsognathus (prō komp′ s*o*g na′ th*u*s; *pro* before + *Compsognathus*, which see). An Upper Triassic coelurosaur of primitive aspect.

Prosaurolophus (prō saw′ r*o* lō′ f*u*s; *pro* before + *sauros* reptile + *lophus* crest). An Upper Cretaceous hadrosaur with a small solid crest. From Alberta. Oldman Formation.

Prosauropoda (prō' saw rop' *o* d*a; pro* before + *sauros* reptile + *podos* foot). A suborder of saurischian dinosaurs dominantly of late Triassic age.

Protoceratops (prō' tō ser' *a* tops; *protos* first + *keratos* horn + *ops* face). A small, early ceratopsian lacking horns but with a well-developed frill. From the Cretaceous of Mongolia. Djadochta Formation.

Psittacosaurus (sit' *a* kō saw' r*us; psittakos* parrot + *sauros* reptile). A small ornithischian dinosaur, probably ancestral to the ceratopsians, from the Lower Cretaceous of Mongolia. Ondai Sair Formation.

Pterosauria (te r*o* saw' rē *a; pteron* wing + *sauros* reptile). The flying reptiles, of Jurassic and Cretaceous age.

Rhamphorhynchus (ram f*o* rin' k*us; rhamphos* bill + *rhynchos* snout). An Upper Jurassic pterosaur, or flying reptile, from southern Germany. Solnhofen limestone.

Rutiodon (rut' ē *o* don; *rhytis* wrinkle + *odon* tooth). A phytosaur from the Upper Triassic of western North America.

Rhoetosaurus (rē t*o* saw' r*us. Rhoetus* one of the Gigantes, in Greek mythology + *sauros* reptile). A Lower Jurassic sauropod from Australia.

Saurischia (saw ris' kē *a; sauros* reptile + *ischion* hip). One of the two orders of dinosaurs, characterized by a pelvis in which the pubic bone is directed forwardly and down.

Saurolophus (saw r*o* lō' f*us; sauros* reptile + *lophos* crest). A hadrosaur found in Upper Cretaceous beds both in North America and Asia. Characterized by a spine projecting up from the top of the skull. From the Edmonton Formation of Alberta and the Nemegt Formation of Mongolia.

Sauropoda (saw rop' *o* d*a; sauros* reptile + *podos* foot). A suborder of saurischian dinosaurs, the members of which are typically of gigantic size.

Saurornithoides (sawr awr' ni thoi' dēz; *sauros* reptile + *ornithos* bird + *oides* resembling). A small Upper Cretaceous theropod from Mongolia; the last of the deinonychosaurs. Djadochta Formation.

Scelidosaurus (sel' *i* dō saw' r*us; skelidos* rib + *sauros* reptile). A primitive Lower Jurassic armored dinosaur from England. Liassic beds.

Scolosaurus (skō' lō saw' r*us; skolos* thorn + *sauros* reptile). An Upper Cretaceous armored dinosaur from Alberta. Oldman Formation.

Scutellosaurus (skū tel' ō saw' r*us; scutellum* little shield + *sauros* reptile). A small, armored ornithischian of late Triassic or early Jurassic age, from northern Arizona. Kayenta Formation.

Shantungosaurus (shan tung ō saw' r*us; Shantung* a Chinese province + *sauros* reptile). The largest of the hadrosaurs, from the Upper Cretaceous of China. Campanian beds.

Spinosaurus (spī n*o* saw' r*us; spina* spine + *sauros* reptile). An Upper Cretaceous carnosaur of large size, with elongated vertebral spines. From Egypt. Baharia Formation.

Stegoceras (steg' ō ser' *as; stegos* roof + *keras* horn). A small, Upper Cretaceous pachycephalosaur, or dome-headed dinosaur, from Montana and Alberta. Judith River and Oldman formations.

Stegosauria (steg' ō saw' rē *a; stegos* roof + *sauros* reptile). A suborder of ornithischian dinosaurs; the "plated" dinosaurs.

Stegosaurus (steg' ō saw' r*us; stegos* roof + *sauros* reptile). A large Upper Jurassic ornithischian, with a double row of plates along the back, from western North America. Morrison Formation.

Struthiomimus (stroo' thē ō mī' m*us; struthion* ostrich + *mimos* mimic). A lightly built, Upper Cretaceous theropod from Alberta in which the jaws are toothless, and form a bird-like beak. Oldman formation.

Styracosaurus (stī rak' ō saw' r*us; styrakion* end of a spear + *sauros* reptile). An Upper Cretaceous ceratopsian distinguished by large spikes along the edge of the frill, from Montana and Alberta. Judith River and Oldman formations.

Syntarsus (sin tär' sis; *syn* together + *tarsos* flat of the foot). A small Upper Triassic theropod from southern Africa, closely related to *Coelophysis* from New Mexico. Forest Sandstone Formation.

Tarbosaurus (tär' bō saw' r*us; tarbos* fear + *sauros* reptile). A gigantic Upper Cretaceous carnosaur from Mongolia, closely related to the North American *Tyrannosaurus*. Nemegt Formation.

Tenontosaurus (ten on' tō saw' r*us; tenontos* sinew + *sauros* reptile). A Lower Cretaceous ornithopod from Montana. Lakota Formation.

Thecodontia (thē' kō don' tē *a; theke* sheath + *odon* tooth). An order of archosaurian reptiles of Triassic age; ultimately ancestral to the crocodiles, dinosaurs, and pterosaurs.

Therapsida (th*e* rap' si d*a; theros* wild beast + *apsidos* arch). The mammal-like reptiles.

Theropoda (th*e* rop' *o* d*a; theros* wild beast + *podos* foot). A suborder of saurischian dinosaurs. This is the one group of carnivorous dinosaurs.

Triceratops (trī ser' *a* tops; *treis* three + *keratos* horn + *ops* face). Perhaps the best known of the ceratopsians and one of the last of the dinosaurs. From western North America. Lance and Hell Creek formations.

Tritylodontia (trī til' *o* don' tē *a; treis* three + *tylos* knob + *odon* tooth). An advanced group of mammal-like reptiles, from the Upper Triassic and Lower Jurassic of Africa, North America, South America, Europe, and Asia.

Toujiangosaurus (too jon gō saw′ rus; *Toujiang* a river in Szechuan, China + *sauros* reptile). A stegosaur from Szechuan, characterized by numerous plates along the back. Upper Jurassic.

Tsintaosaurus (tsin tä ō saw′ rus; *Tsintao* a city in Shantung, China + *sauros* reptile). An Upper Cretaceous hadrosaur with a large, upright spike on the skull. Wangsi Formation.

Typothorax (tī′ pō thaw′ rax; *typos* impression + *thorax* breast plate). An Upper Triassic armored thecodont from southwestern United States. Chinle Formation.

Tyrannosaurus (ti ran′ o saw′ rus; *tyrannos* despot + *sauros* reptile). A gigantic Upper Cretaceous theropod from Montana; the largest of the carnivorous dinosaurs. Hell Creek Formation.

Velociraptor (ve los *i* rap′ tawr; *velocis* swift + *rapere* to plunder or rob). A small Upper Cretaceous theropod from Mongolia. Djadochta Formation.

Credits

The illustrations in this book, noted by page number,
are used with the express permission of the sources listed.

220

96–7, 102, 121, 130, 131, 136–7, 138, 162–3. Zdeněk Burian, 1972. By permission ARTIA Publishers, Praha, Czechoslovakia.

99. "*Archaeopteryx* and the origin of birds," John H. Ostrom (1976), Biological Journal of the Linnaean Society, Vol. 8, pp 91–182.

113 (top and middle). From Lull, Richards and Wright, 1942.

124. From Hatcher, J. B., Marsh, O. C., and Lull, R. S., 1907. Monograph, U.S. Geological Survey, Vol.49, p 45.

134, 135. From Przygody a skamienialym swiecie by Zofia Kielan-Jaworowska, 1973, Warsaw.

159. From Gilmore, C. W., 1914. Smithsonian Institution, U.S. National Museum, Bulletin 89, plate 12.

172, 173. Edwin H. Colbert and the Museum of Northern Arizona.

183. From H. F. Osborn, Bulletin of the American Museum of Natural History, Vol. 20, p 189, 1904.

206. By J. David Archibald, from "Late Cretaceous Extinctions," *American Scientist*, 70: 377–85.

INDEX

Page numbers in italics refer to illustrations and their captions;
* indicates a restoration, showing the animal as it might have appeared in life.